EARLY TRAVELLERS IN
NORTH AMERICA

*Eyewitness Reports from the First
Visitors to the New World*

Early Travellers in
North America

*Eyewitness Reports from the First
Visitors to the New World*

CHARLES MILLER

ALAN SUTTON PUBLISHING LIMITED

First published in the United Kingdom in 1994
Alan Sutton Publishing Limited
Phoenix Mill · Far Thrupp · Stroud · Gloucestershire

First published in the United States of America in 1994
Alan Sutton Publishing Inc
83 Washington Street · Dover · NH 03820

Copyright © Charles Miller, 1994

All rights reserved. No part of this publication may be reproduced, stored in a retrieval system, or transmitted, in any form, or by any means, electronic, mechanical, photocopying, recording or otherwise, without the prior permission of the publishers and copyright holder.

British Library Cataloguing-in-Publication Data

A catalogue record for this book is available from the British Library.

ISBN 0–7509–0478–X (case)
     0–7509–0744–4 (paper)

Library of Congress Cataloging-in-Publication Data applied for

Typeset in 11/15pt Bembo.
Typesetting and origination by
Alan Sutton Publishing Limited.
Printed in Great Britain by
Butler and Tanner, Frome, Somerset.

London Borough
of Enfield
Arts And Libraries

*To my wife Beccy and my mother Katharine,
remembering happy times in Ontario*

The more I see of the Americans, the more plainly I see how great and lamentable an ignorance of each other the people of two continents may live in, in spite of all the modern facilities of communication.

GEORGE BORRETT, LONDON, 1866

CONTENTS

ACKNOWLEDGEMENTS ix

INTRODUCTION xi

Chapter One – SKIMMING THE SURFACE 1
    First impressions – Physical appearance of Americans – Their manner to strangers – Visits at home – Questioning of foreigners – 'How do you like America?' – Discussion of Britain – National climates compared – British boasts

Chapter Two – BED AND BOARD 19
    American hotel breakfast – Dinner and tea – American table manners – The bar – Water and ice – Booking a hotel room – Scale and efficiency of hotels – No privacy in backwoods' inns – A fight in a dormitory at Victoria

Chapter Three – A MANNER OF SPEAKING 33
    American expressions – 'Go the Whole Hog' – Language of the railroad – Captain Marryat's guide to American usage – 'Um, hu' – Accents, English and regional – Place-names, classical and Indian – Future of American English

Chapter Four – ON THE ROAD 43
    Americans and travel – Corduroy roads – Bruises of stage-coach ride – Steamboats – Danger of explosions – A luxurious railway carriage – Passengers' clothes set on fire – The cow-catcher – The conductor – Achievements of the railroad

Chapter Five – NEW SOCIETIES 55
    Indulgence of children – Casual attitude to death – Informality in court – Diversity of religions – The camp meeting – Regional identities – The East – The West – The South – Canada compared to the United States

Chapter Six – A VIEW FROM THE SETTLEMENTS 69
    Emigrants for sale – Arrival at the new home – A clearing in the forest – Unhappiness of women settlers – Keys to prosperity – Life of the Oxbridge bachelors – The 'raising bee' – A return from the backwoods

Chapter Seven – AMERICAN LANDSCAPES 81
    A walk in the 'eternal forest' – Uniformity of uncleared trees – Demolition of the forest – Stumps – Rapid development – A Pennsylvania Eden – The fertile prairies – An American seascape – Responding to nature

Chapter Eight – INDIANS 90
    Dickens meets a chief – Friendship of settlers and Indians – Indians discover maps – Ragged Indians seen from the train – Cruelty of white civilization to Indians – Scalping – Brandy – Future of the Indians

Chapter Nine – SLAVES 100
    First encounters with slaves – A plantation infirmary – British visitors deceived by American slave owners – Affection between slaves and owners – Slave auction – Slavery in the land of liberty – Death of a slave

Chapter Ten – THE DANGERS OF DEMOCRACY 112
    Monarchy and republicanism – A visit to Congress – Meeting the President – Familiarity and democracy – Equality, in trains and hotels – Servility and independence – Backwoods' servants – Benefits of the American political system

Chapter Eleven – A NEW WORLD FOR WOMEN 123
    Appearance of American women – Regional variations – Transience of beauty – Clothes and make-up – Safety of female travellers – Women and politics – Female conversation – Need for women's contribution to society

Chapter Twelve – A GAZETTEER OF EASTERN ADVANCEMENT 133
    New York – Boston – Baltimore – Philadelphia – Washington – Portland – Quebec – Montreal – Hamilton – London – Niagara Falls

Chapter Thirteen – A GAZETTEER OF WESTERN DEVELOPMENT 153
    Toronto – Chicago – Cincinnati – Detroit – Cleveland – Milwaukee – Buffalo – Winnipeg – St Paul – Calgary – Victoria – Vancouver – San Francisco – Monterey – Los Angeles – San Diego

Chapter Fourteen – WRITING AND OTHER BUSINESS 167
    Pleasures and rewards of the lecture circuit – Effect of writers on their company – Honesty of first impressions – Dangers of caricature – Reactions to Mrs Trollope – Anthony Trollope's disappointment – Predictions

Chapter Fifteen – HOME AND ABROAD 177
    Home thoughts from abroad – Patriotism of the emigrant – Homesickness of the visitor – Sadness at leaving America – Praise for North Americans – Admiration for democratic system – Home, seen in a new light

APPENDIX ONE – The Writers and their Journeys 186

APPENDIX TWO – Chronology of Visits and Current Events 193

APPENDIX THREE – British Impressions of America, Past and Present 195

BIBLIOGRAPHY 197

PICTURE AND COPYRIGHT CREDITS 199

INDEX 200

Acknowledgements

Before I had a chance to write this book, some of the ingredients I had collected for it were used in a BBC television series. I would like to thank my colleagues at the BBC who contributed to what appears here in many ways. In particular, Caroline Wright, Associate Producer of the series, unearthed some of the historical material while preparing the television scripts. And Tess Weightman researched the pictures for both the series and the book; her expertise and organization were invaluable.

I would also like to thank my friends Steve and Noreen McDonald in Barrie, Ontario, with whom I have enjoyed many visits to Canada over almost twenty years; they inspired me with a love of their country which led to the collection of a shelf of nineteenth-century travellers' journals on which this book is based.

I hope Steve and Noreen and other Canadian and American friends will see the book as contributing to understanding between our cultures, and not simply as a celebration of British prejudice about North America. There is plenty of that in the writers quoted here, but it is revived for entertainment rather than to give offence. If it is not funny, then its interest today lies as much in what it reveals about its writers as in its depiction of North America.

INTRODUCTION

Today's visitor to North America finds it not so much a strange land as a strangely familiar one. A well-entertained foreigner can identify most of the landmarks of central Manhattan before having been there. The culture has been so thoroughly circulated in movies and advertisements, on television and in books, that visitors' postcards are now less about discovery than recognition, of expectations fulfilled or disappointed.

There was a market for news about North America long before its fame was spread by modern media. Europeans wanted to know whether they should emigrate, or what kind of a life their family or friends had found across the Atlantic; anyone thinking of undertaking the long and often hazardous journey, even if only on a business trip or for pleasure, would be anxious for information. The interpretation of North America by Europeans for a European audience has been a small industry for over a century: the land of new arrivals spawned a literature of first impressions.

It is largely a literature of innocence and honesty, driven by a desire to record significant experiences in detail as they happen. The visitor lives life faster and more fully than at home. Everything must be recorded today to be recollected accurately in more peaceful times. On another level, the accounts of British visitors, in particular, are more than simple travelogues: competition between Britain and America, as well as their close relationship, gives every observation a political dimension. Pride, resentment, indignation and ridicule are never far below the surface of an apparently factual record.

Europeans and North Americans still regard each other with a mixture of affection and suspicion. To those North Americans whose family home was once in Europe, today's Europeans are rather more pleased with themselves than their recent achievements should merit. (A Washington journalist complaining about the influence of the British magazine *The Economist* in the States, asked 'Who are the British, of all people, to lecture us about economics?') Europeans visiting Canada or the United States find themselves in societies which, in many ways, seem to work better than their own: there is more space, more money, and, apparently, more opportunity. And yet the grudging European, who, when home, most enjoys drinking and watching television, can be heard complaining about the 'lack of history'.

This book compiles the collected impressions of fifty British travellers in the last century who wrote accounts of people, places, and customs as they found them in Canada and the United States. Some had emigrated and were writing home to members of their family, who eventually published their accounts. Others were commissioned to travel in order to write a book. A third group were tourists, out to satisfy their curiosity about the New World. All of them were interpreting what they saw for an audience who had never been to America.

There is no shortage of British accounts of North America written both before and after those selected here. But earlier accounts were often written by explorers, whose observations contain less that can be compared with the experience of North America today. And later writers took for granted some of the more common American experiences (such as going to a bar for a drink) which were once sufficiently unknown in Britain to need describing in detail. Even during the century, writers began to assume their readers were familiar with some of their material. Accounts of the inside of American trains, or the view of Niagara Falls were included with the hint of an apology ('as is generally known', or some such formula).

The 1800s were a time of enormous change in the United States and Canada, but it is not the purpose of this book to compare accounts from early in the century with those written later. Such material certainly exists, as some of the writers themselves noticed: in 1895, for instance, Lady Theodora Guest, having read Charles Dickens' journal of his travels fifty years earlier, commented on the improved railway service:

We started afresh, and sat outside the car enjoying the ninety-mile journey to Philadelphia, which was accomplished in about two hours and a half. In amusing contrast is the sentence in C. Dickens's diary in 1842, when he says: 'The journey from New York to Philadelphia is made by railroad, and two ferries, and usually occupies between five and six hours.'

There were many more dramatic changes than this; but there were also both trivial and deep-rooted features of life in North America which remained the same and provoked a similar reaction from British visitors throughout the century. Some are still commented on by the British today: indifference to large distances, the emphasis on making money, the Americans' lack of reserve, and the large amount of food offered at meals, remain the clichés of the Briton who has returned from a trip across the Atlantic. This last point, for example, was made by one of the earliest of these travellers, William Cobbett in 1817, comparing the generous hospitality of Americans with the stinginess of British hosts, whose looks, he said, seem to tell guests 'don't eat too much':

It is not thus that you are received in America. You are not much asked, not much pressed, to eat and drink; but, such an abundance is spread before you, and so hearty and so cordial is your reception, that you instantly lose all restraint, and are tempted to feast whether you are hungry or not.

Finally, two small notes: Canadians are understandably irritated to hear themselves described carelessly as 'American'; unfortunately, many British writers who included Canada in their travels made general observations about 'America', and there is no particular reason to think they were mentally excluding what they had seen in Canada. I have used the phrase 'North America' to include both Canada and the United States, but in some cases, I too will ask my readers to take 'American' as an abbreviation for 'North American'. Secondly, I have only made internal cuts in the quoted material after the usual three dots; in some cases I have updated spelling, but I have left the punctuation as it was, including what today seems like an unreasonable number of commas.

CHAPTER ONE

SKIMMING THE SURFACE

How in the world was it possible to take in even one-thousandth of this huge, roaring, many-sided continent?

RUDYARD KIPLING

The curiosity with which trans-Atlantic passengers peer down onto the suburbs of New York through the windows of a descending 747 can be nothing to the expectations of those who disembarked after several weeks at sea in the last century. Even today, most Europeans who arrive in North America have never before been further from home and are visiting a country unimaginably larger than their own. A hundred years ago, such travellers would be gambling months or years of their lives, and often all their worldly wealth on travelling to America. No wonder, then, that they were anxious to discover whether the reality of the New World would match its reputation.

As the continent appeared on the horizon, passengers would stare at the coastline, and later, after the thrill of arriving in harbour, at the people in the city streets. For the British, everything was new, and yet there was also much that was familiar. Was America essentially the same as their own country, or would closer examination reveal subtle and interesting differences?

Henry Bradshaw Fearon, an Englishman on board the *Washington*, as it picked up a pilot to navigate into New York harbour in 1817, scrutinized the scene: 'every object was to me an interesting one: first our pilot, his stature, his manners, his dress, were all, at this time, objects of my attention; though under different circumstances I should have viewed them with entire indifference.'

Fearon had been commissioned by a group of English families who were considering emigration, to survey the prospects for their various trades in the States and to provide, as he said, 'that homely kind of intelligence which was wanted on such an occasion'. He took his job seriously, providing exhaustive lists of prices, and noting down everything he saw, starting on the first day, on the streets of New York:

'England has already declined, since she has lost the States; and to these States, therefore, yet undeveloped, full of dark possibilities, and grown, like another Eve, from one rib out of the side of their own land, the minds of young men in England turn naturally at a certain hopeful period of their age.'

ROBERT LOUIS STEVENSON

The street population bears an aspect essentially different from that of London, or large English towns. One striking feature consists in the number of blacks, many of whom are finely dressed, the females very ludicrously so, showing a partiality to white muslin dresses, artificial flowers, and pink shoes. I saw but few well-dressed white ladies . . . The dress of the men is rather deficient in point of neatness and gentility. Their appearance, in common with that of the ladies and children, is sallow, and what we should call unhealthy.

Each of the millions of British and Irish emigrants who arrived in the nineteenth century must have looked just as closely at the scene that greeted them, searching for clues by which to interpret America. As transport became faster and more reliable, the emigrants were joined by increasing numbers of tourists, who needed only a certain amount of money and luck to enjoy a reasonably comfortable tour of the States and Canada. According to the novelist Anthony Trollope in 1861, two months and £120 would allow a satisfactory tour with 'wine, washing and other luxuries'.

While Fearon concluded after his first day that the people of New York were 'essentially different', others recorded, with disappointment, that New Yorkers were less exotic than they had hoped:

> The appearance of the population, though not English, is undoubtedly nearer to it than that of any city on the continent of Europe; and but for the number of blacks and people of colour, one encounters in the streets, there is certainly little to remind a traveller that the breadth of an ocean divides him from Great Britain.
>
> THOMAS HAMILTON

Captain Hamilton had retired from the Army and written a successful novel, *Cyril Thornton*, whose popularity in the United States, he told his brother when he arrived, made him 'a bit of a lion, and the object of much more notice than is desirable'. His celebrity gained him entry to the smartest circles, and his account of his tour in 1830, *Men and Manners in America*, is one of amusement at the excesses of American society.

Two other seafaring captains offered their first impressions of New York, both describing rather precisely the combination of familiarity and strangeness which first strikes a European visitor:

> As we passed along, many things recalled the seaports of England to my thoughts, although abundant indications of another country lay on all hands. The signs over the shop doors were written in English; but the language we heard spoken was different in tone from what we had been accustomed to . . . The whole seemed at times, more like a dream than a sober reality. For there was so much about it that looked like England, that we half fancied ourselves back again; and yet there was quite enough to show in the next instant, that it was a very different country. This indistinct, dreamy kind of feeling, lasted for several days; after which it gradually faded away before a different set of impressions, which will be described in their turn.
>
> BASIL HALL

Captain Hall had already written successfully about his naval trips. His *Travels in North America*, published in 1829, was one of the first British journals to give offence to Americans. He was widely quoted by later writers, confirming or denying his conclusions.

Another retired seaman, Captain Frederick Marryat, author of over thirty popular novels including *Mr Midshipman Easy*, described how, during his first weeks in New York in 1837, he began to develop a sense of what was truly American:

> On my first arrival I perceived little difference between the city of New York and one of our principal provincial towns; and, for its people, not half so much as between the people

'I never saw an American man walk or stand well; notwithstanding their frequent militia drillings, they are nearly all hollow chested and round shouldered.'

FANNY TROLLOPE

of Devonshire or Cornwall and those of Middlesex. I had been two or three weeks in that city, and I said: There is certainly not much to write about . . . But in a short time I altered my opinion: even at New York, the English appearance of the people gradually wore away; my perception of character became more keen, my observance consequently more nice and close, and I found that there was a great deal to reflect upon and investigate, and that America and the American people were indeed an enigma.

Charles Kingsley summed up the first impressions of many Britons when he described Americans as 'English, with a difference'. Some writers tried to define that difference, beginning with a study of physique: Thomas Hamilton described Americans as 'generally slender in person, somewhat slouching in gait, and without that openness of countenance and erectness of deportment to which an English eye has been accustomed'. Others, such as Fanny Trollope, offered a more ambitious analysis:

I never saw an American man walk or stand well; notwithstanding their frequent militia drillings, they are nearly all hollow chested and round shouldered: perhaps this is occasioned by no officer daring to say to a brother free-born 'hold up your head;' whatever the cause, the effect is very remarkable to a stranger. In stature, and in physiognomy, a great majority of the population, both male and female, are strikingly handsome, but they know not how to do their own honours; half as much comeliness elsewhere would produce ten times as much effect.

Mrs Trollope, mother of the novelist Anthony Trollope, was the middle-aged wife of an unsuccessful barrister when she went to America in 1827, leaving the twelve-year-old Anthony in England. She was planning to help in a Tennessee community for the education of former slaves, but abandoned the idea when she found conditions in the project's forest clearing too primitive. She opened a boutique in Cincinnati, but the business failed; to pay her debts she turned to writing. Her indignant, anecdotal *Domestic Manners of the Americans* was unflattering enough about its subjects to become a best-seller, saving her family from financial ruin.

Like Mrs Trollope, Captain Marryat also claimed that Americans were in a peculiar way responsible for their own unattractive appearance:

As I walked down Broadway, it appeared strange to me that there should be such a remarkable family likeness among the people. Every man I met seemed to me by his features to be a brother or a connection of the last man who had passed me; I could not at first comprehend this, but the mystery was soon revealed. It was that they were all intent and engrossed with the same object; all were, as they passed, calculating and reflecting; this produced a similar contraction of the brow, knitting of the eyebrows, and compression of the lips – a similarity of feeling had produced a similarity of expression, from the same muscles being called into action.

William Howard Russell, a foreign correspondent for the London *Times*, strolled down Broadway and summarized the typical features of the men he saw: 'straight hair, keen, bright, penetrating eyes, and want of colour in the cheeks'. This pallor in North American faces, both male and female, was often noted, and compared to the 'rosy cheeks' of the British. Susanna Moodie, a middle-class Englishwoman who emigrated to the backwoods of Canada in 1832, was sensitive to the prevailing tastes in female beauty:

The rosy face of the British emigrant is regarded as no beauty here. The Canadian women, like their neighbours the Americans, have small regular features, but are mostly pale, or their faces are only slightly suffused with a faint flush. During the season of youth this delicate tinting is very beautiful, but a few years deprive them of it, and leave a sickly, sallow pallor in its place.

Moodie attributed the effect to 'the withering influence of late hours and stove-heat'. Anthony Trollope, making his own tour of North America thirty years after his mother, came to the same conclusion about the pale faces of America:

As to the hot-air pipes, there can, I think be no doubt that to them is to be charged the murder of all rosy cheeks throughout the States. If the effect was to be noticed simply in the dry faces of the men about Wall Street, I should be very indifferent to the matter. But the young ladies of Fifth Avenue are in the same category. The very pith and marrow of life is baked out of their young bones by the hot-air chambers to which they are accustomed. Hot air is the great destroyer of American beauty.

The new arrival, having surveyed the population and commented on its appearance, next ventured to make contact. Thomas Hamilton asked New Yorkers for directions, and reported mixed reactions:

I found it necessary to ask my way, and accordingly entered a small grocer's shop. 'Pray sir,' I said, 'can you point out to me the way to Niblo's tavern?' The person thus addressed was rather a gruff-looking man, in a scratch-wig, and for at least half a minute kept eyeing me from top to toe without uttering a syllable. 'Yes, sir, I can,' he at length replied, with a stare as broad as if he had taken me for the great Katterfelto. Considering this sort of treatment, as the mere ebullition of republican insolence, I was in the act of turning on my heel and quitting the shop, when the man added, 'and I shall have great pleasure in showing it to you.' He then crossed the counter, and accompanying me to the middle of the street, pointed out the land-marks by which I was to steer, and gave the most minute direction for my guidance . . . This incident afforded me the first practical insight into the manners of the people . . . Had my impulse to quit the shop been executed with greater rapidity, I should certainly have considered this man as a brutal barbarian, and perhaps have drawn an unfair inference with regard to the manners and character, of the lower orders of society in the United States.

In 1879 Robert Louis Stevenson found himself in New York on his way to California, where he was joining Fanny Osbourne, an American he had met and fallen in love with in France. Stevenson disembarked in New York, and had just one rainy day to organize himself for a gruelling train journey across the continent. In his dealings in the city, he found the same kind of contrariness described by Hamilton:

Wherever I went, the same traits struck me: the people were all surprisingly rude and surprisingly kind. The money-changer cross-questioned me like a French commissary, asking my age, my business, my average income, and my destination, beating down my attempts at evasion, and receiving my answers in silence; and yet when all was over, he shook hands with me up to the elbows, and sent his lad nearly a quarter of a mile in the rain to get me books at a reduction. Again, in a very large publishing and bookselling establishment a man, who seemed to be the manager, received me as I had certainly never before been received in any human shop, indicated squarely that he put no faith in my honesty, and refused to look up the names of books or give me the slightest help of information, on the ground, like the steward, that it was none of his business. I lost my temper at last, said I was a stranger in America and not learned in their etiquette; but I would assure him, if he went to any bookseller in England, of more handsome usage. The boast was perhaps exaggerated; but like many a long shot, it struck the gold. The manager passed at once from one extreme to the other; I may say that from that moment he loaded me with kindness; he gave me all sorts of good advice, wrote me down addresses, and came bareheaded into the rain to point me out a restaurant, where I might lunch, nor even then did he seem to think that he had done enough. These are (it is as well to be bold in statement) the manners of America.

Initial encounters, then, were a strange mixture of bluntness and generosity. Rude, or at least undeferential, questioning was shortly followed by kindness and help. Further experience revealed the same lack of reserve in most dealings with Americans; to the British, this informal style was a novelty. Henry Bradshaw Fearon described American manners as 'more easy, but less polite' than British. Manifestations of such social ease were initially disconcerting, according to Captain Marryat:

When you travel, or indeed when walking the streets in the western country, if you have a cigar in your mouth, a man will come up – 'Beg pardon, stranger,' and whips your cigar out of your mouth, lights his own, and then returns yours. I thought it rather cool at first, but as I found it was the practice, I invariably did the same whenever I needed a light.

Amelia Murray was an aristocratic young Englishwoman on tour in 1854. From a hotel overlooking Niagara Falls she reported several incidents which led her to conclude that Americans 'mistake rudeness for republicanism, and incivility for independence':

I was busy making a little sketch from the veranda, when I felt a hand familiarly laid upon my shoulder. Of course I supposed it was a lady with whom I had some acquaintance, but when a strange voice asked a question, I turned round: it was with no small degree of astonishment that I found the liberty was taken by a perfect stranger . . . She did not seem the least daunted by the expression of surprise which must have passed over my face, but went on questioning me with the coolest manner imaginable!

Fanny Trollope was surprised to receive uninvited visits from local people whom she had never met. It was, she reported, unacceptable to fasten one's door in Cincinnati, and such visits were 'most vexatious interruptions' to her family's domestic life. The visitors would seat themselves in the living-room, and expect Mrs Trollope to continue with her activities while they looked on for an hour or more. Conversation was not required: 'at length, rising abruptly, they would again shake hands, with, "Well, now I must be going, I guess" and so take themselves off, apparently well contented with their reception.'

Further from urban society, even greater assumptions were made about the rights of visitors in one's home, as Susanna Moodie's sister and fellow settler in Canada, Catherine Parr Traill, discovered:

When I lived in the backwoods, out of sight of any other habitation, the door has often been opened at midnight, a stranger has entered and lain down before the kitchen fire, and departed in the morning unquestioned . . . What a contrast to my home in England, where by sunset every door was secured with locks and heavy bars and bolts . . . The approach of a stranger was beheld with suspicion; and however great his need, we dared not afford him the shelter of our roof, lest our so doing should open the door to robber or murderer. At first I could hardly understand why it happened that I never felt the same sensation of fear in Canada as I had done in England. My mind seemed lightened of a heavy burden; and I, who had been so timid, grew brave and fearless amid the gloomy forests of Canada.

At all levels of society, this relaxation of behaviour, and crossing of British boundaries was found. Partly as a foreigner, and partly as a well-known writer, Charles Dickens was the subject of curiosity which, in Britain, would have been politely concealed. One evening in 1842 on his lecture tour of the States, he was in a train waiting to leave Baltimore:

Those men and boys who happened to have nothing particular to do, and were curious in foreigners, came (according to custom) round the carriage in which I sat; let down all the windows; thrust in their heads and shoulders; hooked themselves on conveniently, by their elbows; and fell to comparing notes on the subject of my personal appearance, with as much indifference as if I were a stuffed figure. I never gained so much uncompromising information with reference to my own nose and eyes, the various impressions wrought by my mouth and chin on different minds, and how my head looks when it is viewed from behind, as on these occasions. Some gentlemen were only satisfied by exercising their sense

THE WRITERS

CHARLES DICKENS (1812–70) went to America with his wife in 1842, hoping to write a book that would present a more favourable view of its society than that of previous travellers. Dickens was only thirty, but already well known for *Pickwick Papers* (1836), *Oliver Twist* (1837) and other novels. He was greeted in Boston with hundreds of requests for meetings and autographs, and met American writers including Irving, Longfellow, Lowell and Dana. Indeed, his social life became so complicated that he employed a secretary and was soon cancelling engagements from sheer exhaustion. He wrote home: 'I can do nothing that I want to do, go nowhere where I want to go, and see nothing that I want to see. If I turn into a street, I am followed by a multitude. If I stay at home, the house becomes, with callers, like a fair.' Nevertheless, Dickens managed to visit institutions – hospitals, factories, universities – and form a picture of American life which he captured in *American Notes for General Circulation* (1842). He was enthusiastic, toasting at a public dinner to 'America and England – and may they never have any division but the Atlantic between them'. But he was less popular with his American hosts for raising the awkward question of copyright: British writers at the time received nothing from their American sales. And as his tour took him away from the refinement of New England, he came upon the features of American life which previous accounts had criticized: spitting, overcharging at hotels, the crudeness of American newspapers, slavery. He was left with the same complicated, contradictory feelings of other writers, torn between outrage at some of what he had seen, and true affection and admiration for many of those he had met and befriended. 'I can scarcely be supposed to be ignorant of the hazard I run in writing of America at all,' he wrote; 'I know perfectly well that there is, in that country, a numerous class of well-intentioned persons prone to be dissatisfied with all accounts of the Republic whose citizens they are, which are not couched in terms of exalted and extravagent praise.'

of touch; and the boys (who are surprisingly precocious in America) were seldom satisfied, even by that, but would return to the charge over and over again. Many a budding president has walked into my room with his cap on his head and his hands in his pockets, and stared at me for two whole hours: occasionally refreshing himself with a tweak of his nose, or a draught from the water-jug.

Other writers felt similarly invaded:

A man's person in America is, like everything else, public property. Should you be wearing anything curious in the way of coats, you will be sure to have two or three fingers and thumbs trying its texture; and if any one takes a fancy to your trousers he will test them in a similar way, and ask you if you've 'a mind to trade them' . . . I am told that a Yankee has been seen to raise a man's hat from his head to read the maker's name inside. Was there ever such a land of freedom! Why, at home, it would be assault and battery.

GEORGE BORRETT

Borrett, a fellow of King's College, Cambridge, described his tour of Canada and the United States in 1864 in letters to his family; like many other writers, he allowed his correspondence to be published when friends persuaded him it would be popular with a wider readership.

Another rather smart English traveller, Clara Bromley, wrote home to her father, a knight and a member of parliament; her letters were published in 1861 as *A Woman's Wanderings in the Western World*. Bromley brought a refreshingly open-minded approach to the question of personal privacy:

I am never inclined either to think or treat this inquisitiveness as an impertinence, and, moreover, I do not think they mean it themselves as such; I believe it arises from their desire to compare themselves, their sayings and doings, with every stranger they come across, and in their anxiety to do this, they occasionally lose sight of the bounds of good breeding. On the other hand we English go into an opposite extreme. The indifference with which we view everybody we do not know, the fright we are in lest we should know some one who is not as high up as ourselves in the social scale. And as to asking questions!

Thomas Hamilton found himself under scrutiny at smart dinner parties, but he too learnt to accept the approach:

I admit there is a . . . even bluntness in American manners, somewhat startling at first to a sophisticated European. Questions are asked with regard to one's habits, family, pursuits, connexions, and opinions, which are never put in England, except in a witness box, after the ceremony of swearing on the four Evangelists. But this is done with the most perfect bonhomie, and evidently without the smallest conception, that such an examination can possibly be offensive to the patient.

Hamilton concluded that 'it is scarcely fair to judge one nation by the conventional standard of another', and that the temporary distress of a secretive European is, in the end, a small consideration compared to the attractions of American manners:

> There is a sort of republican plainness and simplicity in their address, quite in harmony with the institutions of their country. An American bows less than an Englishman; he deals less in mere conventional forms and expressions of civility; he pays few or no compliments; makes no unmeaning or overstrained professions; but he takes you by the hand with a cordiality which at once intimates, that he is disposed to regard you as a friend . . . In no other country I have ever visited, are the charities of life so readily and so profusely opened to a stranger as in the United States.

'From a pretty long and intimate acquaintance with American society in most of its phases, I can confidently say, that the traveller who finds the people of America habitually keeping him at a distance, and otherwise treating him coldly, must be himself chiefly to blame for the reception which he experiences.'
ALEXANDER MACKAY

Alexander Mackay, a London barrister, who had set himself the task of exploring the 'social, political, and industrial' development of the United States, was similarly warm: although the British might interpret American behaviour as an 'impudent liberty', they should 'leave their European notions of exclusiveness at home' and accept the offer of friendship.

When British visitors had learnt to tolerate, or even appreciate, American manners, a likely first subject of conversation was almost guaranteed to spoil the atmosphere: any discussion of the merits of Britain or America was a threat to national pride on both sides, and was made even more difficult by a clash between American bluntness and British obfuscation. Comparisons arose because Americans insisted on them: British visitors complained about being pumped for their opinions of America even before setting foot on dry land. As soon as the flat shoreline around Boston was visible, Charles Weld found an American fellow passenger 'passing his arm through mine, and pointing to the thin line of coast scarcely discernible from the sky, asking at the same time whether "that was not fine?" Weld was another English barrister, on a 'vacation tour'; his non-commital response did not satisfy his questioner: 'without compromising my regard for truth, I answered in a manner which I trusted would relieve me from all furthur questions of a like nature; but I was disappointed.'

Also ambushed for a compliment before she had arrived in the country, Harriet Martineau had anticipated the question, but was just as surprised when it first came:

When I was on my voyage out, the Americans on board amused themselves with describing to me how incessantly I should be met by the question how I liked America. When we arrived within a few miles of New York, a steam-boat met us, bringing the friends of some of the passengers. On board this steam-boat, the passengers went up to the city. It happened to be the smallest, dirtiest, and most clumsy steamer belonging to the port. A splashing rain drove us down into the cabin, where there was barely standing room for our company. We saw each other's faces by the dim light of a single shabby lamp. 'Now, Miss M.' said some of the American passengers, 'how do you like America?'

Arriving in America in 1834, Martineau was a well-known intellectual, an economist, novelist, journalist, and writer on religion and travel. Her more considered opinions on the States were, indeed, much sought after, and published in her *Society in America* and a further three volume *Retrospect of Western Travel*.

Like many other travellers, Basil Hall felt that American demands for British opinions were not to be taken as genuine enquiries:

The question, 'What do you think of us upon the whole?' was put to me every day, and almost in every company. But I am sorry that truth compels me to add, that whenever the reply which this abrupt and rather startling question elicited, was not one of unqualified praise, a certain painful degree of dissatisfaction was produced.

Hall was irritated by American boasts ('the constant habit of praising themselves'), and gave the following example of what he claimed was a national sensitivity to the possibility that there might be limits to a British visitor's admiration for America:

I happened one day to mention to a lady, that I had been amused by observing how much more the drivers of the stages managed their horses by word of mouth, than by touch of the whip. Upon which she replied, 'Oh yes, sir, the circumstance you relate is very interesting, as it shows both intelligence in the men, and sagacity in the animals.' This was pretty well;

'The reasons that make the Americans so thin-skinned and touchy about any remark made on their manners and peculiarities are not very dissimilar from those of a boy who has lately taken to stick-up collars and tail-coats; he feels he is not quite a man, though he wishes every one to think so.'

EDWARD SULLIVAN

but I merely smiled and said nothing, being somewhat tickled by this amiable interchange of human wisdom and brute sagacity. The lady's suspicions however instantly took fire on seeing the expression of my countenance, and she answered my smile by saying, 'Nay, sir, do you not think the people in America, upon the whole, particularly intelligent?'

If discussion of America was difficult, the mention of Britain was worse: Hall reported that after any favourable comment about England, 'there was straightaway a fidget, till the said circumstance was counterbalanced by something equally good, or much better, in America.' The usual result was 'a brisk crossfire' of views.

Mrs Trollope recounted many conversations in which, she claimed, she restrained herself from contradicting what was said about Britain:

The favourite, the constant, the universal sneer that met me everywhere, was on our old-fashioned attachments to things obsolete. Had they a little wit among them, I am certain they would have given us the cognomen of 'My Grandmother, the British,' for that is the tone they take, and it is thus they reconcile themselves to the crude newness of every thing around them.

'I wonder you are not sick of kings, chancellors, and archbishops, and all your fustian of wigs and gowns,' said a very clever gentleman to me once, with an affected yawn, 'I protest the very sound almost sends me to sleep.'

Fanny Trollope was later able to put her point of view, to considerable effect, in her book. At the time, her manners were tested to the limit:

I was once sitting with a party of ladies, among whom were one or two young girls, whose curiosity was greater than their patriotism, and they asked me many questions respecting the splendour and extent of London. I was endeavouring to satisfy them by the best description I could give, when we were interrupted by another lady, who exclaimed, 'Do hold your tongues, girls, about London; if you want to know what a beautiful city is, look at Philadelphia; when Mrs Trollope has been there, I think she will allow that it is better worth talking about than that great overgrown collection of nasty, filthy, dirty streets, that they call London.'

When Anthony Trollope toured America, he was surprised to be offered condolences for the sad lack of vegetables in England. He described his way of reducing the chance of hearing such claims:

I have found it expedient to let those with whom I might chance to talk know at once that I was an Englishman. In fault of such knowledge things would be said which could not but be disagreeable to me . . . I have learnt that Wellington was beaten at Waterloo; that Lord Palmerston was so unpopular that he could not walk alone in the streets; that the House of Commons was an acknowledged failure; that starvation was the normal condition of the British people, and that the Queen was a bloodthirsty tyrant.

The most common subject for these international disputes was a British favourite, the weather. Many British visitors recorded their opinion that when it came to storms, the weather in America was altogether more impressive than their own. Charles Weld reported: 'the thunder is louder, and the rain heavier in Canada, than in England.' Rebecca Burland, whose family emigrated to Illinois in 1831, commented on American lightning: 'a person who has lived only in England can have but an imperfect conception of these electrical phenomena.' And Sir Francis Head, a British Governor of Upper Canada, began a book of essays with a lyrical but unpatriotic acknowledgement of the grandeur of nature in North America (later quoted approvingly by the American writer Henry Thoreau):

The heavens of America appear infinitely higher – the sky is bluer – the clouds are whiter – the air is fresher – the cold is intenser – the moon looks larger – the stars are brighter – the thunder is louder – the lightning is vivider - the wind is stronger – the rain is heavier – the mountains are higher – the rivers larger – the forests bigger – the plains broader; in short, the gigantic and beautiful features of the new world seem to correspond very wonderfully with the increased locomotive powers and other brilliant discoveries which, under the blessing of an Almighty power, have lately been developed to mankind.

And yet, the very same observations made by an American sounded like a boast, tempting the British traveller to deny them. Captain Horton Rhys, an amateur actor touring the States and Canada in 1859, was on a train to Montreal which ran into a storm. A fellow traveller struck up conversation:

'Say stranger! – this licks anything you have seen in your country, any way?'
    This remark came from a man – of course, an American – just after a flash had so blinded me, that I had to pass my hand across my eyes to relieve the pain.
    'We whips the world for storms, we does!'
    I really think our companion considered that he had something to do with the uproar of the elements, and was glorified thereby.

Other writers also felt that Americans believed their weather should be as much an object of national pride or shame as their government:

On returning to town, half drowned in the deluges of rain which had been falling all the morning, we were much amused with the apologies made to us, by every one we met, for the state of the weather . . . Almost every person was in the fidgets about the bad weather; not at all on account of its inconvenience either to themselves or to us, – that seemed quite a subordinate consideration, – but purely as it acted against their nationality, by making us suspect their climate was not much better than that of England.

BASIL HALL

A traveller is entreated, nay, sometimes even implored, not to judge of the climate by the specimen he has seen of it. Before his arrival the sky was cloudless, and the atmosphere serene. He has just come in the nick of bad weather. Never, in the memory of the oldest inhabitant, was the snow so deep or so permanent.

THOMAS HAMILTON

The British traveller's professed modesty about British weather ('though attached to the soil of my country, I had really no inclination to vindicate its atmosphere,' said Thomas Hamilton) was perhaps not as general as British accounts would claim; indeed, the British might, in their understated way, just as often, and just as irritatingly, have sung the praises of their country. Henry Bradshaw Fearon quoted an apocryphal story celebrating an American rejoinder to a boastful Briton:

Two Englishmen and an American were travelling in a stage from Boston. The Englishmen indulged their patriotism by abusing every thing American. The butter was not so good as the English – nor the beef – nor the mutton – nor the peaches – nor the laws, nor the people – nor the climate – nor the country. Their fellow-traveller was displeased, but he remained silent. At length there came on a tremendous storm of thunder and lightning. He then burst forth, boiling with rage – 'There, d—— you, I guess that thunder and lightning is as good as any you have in England.'

HENRY BRADSHAW FEARON

Americans were all too familiar with the superior British commentator – 'John Bullism', as William Fraser Rae called it. Rae was a journalist making an early crossing of the continent by rail in 1869. He recorded several stories told him by Americans about objectionable British attitudes:

One of them related how, having paid all the attention in his power to an English fellow-passenger, he naturally expected to hear an expression of admiration for some of the sights pointed out. But he had laboured in vain. Everything was pronounced to be good in its

'The Americans have gained more by their faults having been pointed out by travellers than they will choose to allow.'

CAPTAIN MARRYAT

way, but far inferior to what might be seen in England. In the hope of succeeding at last, he remarked that the moon, which shone so brightly that small print could be read by its light, must rival that of the Old Country. The reply was that the moon was not at all bad for America, yet that the spectacle was far inferior to what is beheld on a moonlight night in England.

If the British boasted about their weather, they must surely have boasted about much else besides. Even British writers who claimed to admire America sometimes revealed as much arrogance as the two Englishmen in the stage-coach. Alexander Mackay concluded, like others, that Americans were over-sensitive to criticism, but excused the trait as the unfortunate result of a succession of hostile reports by his fellow travellers. The British, Mackay explained, would not react so strongly to a few derogatory comments: they naturally found it easier to shrug off criticism, because 'England has her fixed position in the great family of nations, and at the head of civilisation – a position which she has long occupied, and from which it will be some time ere she is driven.' Americans might have found the charge of over-sensitivity easier to swallow than this weighty put-down offered in their defence.

CHAPTER TWO

BED AND BOARD

A poor diet never enters into any combination of circumstances contemplated by an American.

ANTHONY TROLLOPE

FOOD AND DRINK

British visitors were impressed by the quantity, and sometimes the quality of food they were offered in America. But they were surprised to find that meals were accorded as much ceremony as the loading of a pile of logs onto a steamer. Food was a fuel, time was money, and the British were left alone at table long after other diners had departed. Thomas Hamilton provided a comprehensive guide to a day's eating in a New York hotel:

I had nearly completed my toilet on the morning after my arrival, when the tinkling of a large bell gave intimation, that the hour of breakfast was come. I accordingly descended as speedily as possible to the *salle a manger*, and found a considerable party engaged in doing justice to a meal, which, at first glance, one would scarcely have guessed to be a breakfast. Solid viands of all descriptions loaded the table, while, in the occasional intervals, were distributed dishes of rolls, toast, and cakes of buckwheat and Indian corn. At the head of the table, sat the landlady, who, with an air of complacent dignity, was busied in the distribution of tea and coffee. A large bevy of negroes were bustling about, ministering with all possible alacrity, to the many wants which were somewhat vociferously obtruded on their attention.

The contrast of the whole scene, with that of an English breakfast-table, was striking enough. Here was no loitering nor lounging; no dipping into newspapers; no apparent lassitude of appetite; no intervals of repose in mastication; but all was hurry, bustle, clamour, and voracity, and the business of repletion went forward, with a rapidity altogether unexampled. The strenuous efforts of the company were of course, soon rewarded with success. Departures, which had begun even before I took my place at the table, became every instant more numerous . . . The appearance of the table under such circumstances was by no means gracious either to the eye or the fancy. It was thickly strewn with the *disjecta membra* of the entertainment. Here, lay fragments of fish, somewhat unpleasantly odiferous; there, the skeleton of a chicken; on the right, a mustard-pot upset, and the cloth, *passim*, defiled with stains of eggs, coffee, gravy – but I will not go on with the picture.

A substantial breakfast was needed to bridge the long interval to the next meal: dinner was served at three in the afternoon. Once again, Hamilton continued, the guests assembled in the dining-room:

To a gentleman with a keen appetite, the *coup d'oeil* of the dinner-table was far from unpleasing. The number of dishes was very great . . . The dressed dishes were decidedly bad, the sauces being composed of little else than liquid grease, which, to a person like myself, who have an inherent detestation of every modification of oleaginous matter, was an objection altogether insuperable. On the whole, however, it would be unjust to complain. If, as the old adage hath it, 'in the multitude of counsellors there is wisdom', so may it be averred, as equally consistent with human experience, that in the multitude of dishes there is good eating. After several unsuccessful experiments, I did discover unobjectionable viands, and made as good a dinner, as the ambition of an old campaigner could desire.

Around, I beheld the same scene of gulping and swallowing, as if for a wager, which my observations at breakfast had prepared me to expect. In my own neighbourhood there was no conversation. Each individual seemed to *pitchfork* his food down his gullet, without the smallest attention to the wants of his neighbour. If you asked a gentleman to help you from any dish before you, he certainly complied, but in a manner that showed you had imposed on him a disagreeable office; and instead of a *slice*, your plate generally returned loaded with a solid massive wedge of animal matter . . . As the dinner advanced, the party rapidly diminished; before the second course, a considerable portion had taken their departure, and comparatively few waited the appearance of the dessert.

Anthony Trollope was just as startled by hotel eating habits, but less optimistic about finding something he wanted to eat:

How I did learn to hate those little dishes and their greasy contents! At a London eating-house things are often not very nice, but your meat is put on a plate and comes before you in edible shape. At these hotels it is brought to you in horrid little oval dishes, and swims in grease. Gravy is not an institution at American hotels, but grease has taken its place. It is palpable, undisguised grease, floating in rivers, – not grease caused by accidental bad cookery, but grease on purpose. A beef-steak is not a beef-steak unless a quarter of a pound of butter be added to it. Those horrid little dishes!

THE WRITERS

ANTHONY TROLLOPE (1815–82) was beginning his working life as a post office clerk in London in 1834 while his mother was enjoying the success of the book that made her name, *Domestic Manners of the Americans* (1832). He moved to Ireland in 1841, married, and continued to work for the Post Office. Twenty years later, when he had become a valued official, and a successful novelist, having published *The Warden* (1855), *Barchester Towers* (1857) and *Doctor Thorne* (1858) among others, he requested leave of absence from the Post Office to tour America. His trip, starting in 1861, covered both the United States and Canada over nine months, and resulted in a two-volume record, *North America* (1862), written, he remembered in his *Autobiography* (1883) 'almost without a note'. Although, in retrospect, he was not pleased with the book, it demonstrated a genuine effort to be fair, and to analyse impartially the differences between two cultures. Compared to an Englishman, Trollope found an American 'quicker, more universally intelligent, more ambitious of general knowledge, less indulgent of stupidity and ignorance in others, harder, sharper, brighter with the surface brightness of steel'.

There were still two more meals in the day, starting with tea at six o'clock, at which a somewhat smaller crowd would gather:

This meal is likewise provided with its due proportion of solids. The most remarkable was raw hung beef, cut into thin slices, of which, – *horresco referens*, – I observed that even the ladies did not hesitate to partake. The tea and coffee were both execrable. A supper, of cold meat, &c., follows at ten o'clock, and remains on the table till twelve, when eating terminates for the day. Such is the unvarying routine of a New York hotel.

THOMAS HAMILTON

To most British travellers, the table manners of North America were more remarkable than its food. Fanny Trollope reported from a Mississippi steamboat among a party of American military men:

'When a dinner party is given in this country, it is always on a grand scale. Earth, and air, and ocean, are ransacked for their products.'

CAPTAIN HAMILTON

The total want of all the usual courtesies of the table, the voracious rapidity with which the viands were seized and devoured, the strange uncouth phrases and pronunciation; the loathsome spitting, from the contamination of which it was absolutely impossible to protect our dresses; the frightful manner of feeding with their knives, till the whole blade seemed to enter into the mouth; and the still more frightful manner of cleaning their teeth afterwards with a pocket knife, soon forced us to feel that we were not surrounded by the generals, colonels and majors of the old world; and that the dinner hour was to be any thing rather than an hour of enjoyment.

Rudyard Kipling, who first crossed America from west to east on his way to England from his native India, summed up the British view: the American 'has no meals. He stuffs for ten minutes thrice a day.'

British travellers who imagined that mealtimes would offer a chance to introduce themselves to Americans were disappointed:

All attempts to set conversation in motion proved abortive; for each person seemed intent exclusively on the professed business of the meeting, and having dispatched, in all haste, what sustenance was required, and in solemn silence, rose and departed. It might have been thought we had assembled rather for the purpose of inhuming the body of some departed friend, than of merrily keeping alive the existing generation.

BASIL HALL

Charles Dickens, too, on a steamboat to Cincinnati, found that his fellow diners reminded him of death:

All the passengers are very dismal, and seem to have tremendous secrets weighing on their minds. There is no conversation, no laughter, no cheerfulness, no sociality, except in spitting; and that is done in silent fellowship round the stove, when the meal is over. Undertakers on duty would be spritely beside them.

Food, then, at least in public places, was not usually an excuse for entertainment. Drink ('a subject of much more importance in America,' said Captain Marryat), in contrast, lubricated all social and business affairs:

They say that the English cannot settle anything properly without a dinner. I am sure the Americans can fix nothing without a drink. If you meet, you drink; if you part, you drink; if you make acquaintance, you drink; if you close a bargain, you drink; they quarrel in their drink, and they make it up with a drink. They drink because it is hot; they drink because it is cold. If successful in elections, they drink and rejoice; if not, they drink and swear; they begin to drink early in the morning, they leave off late at night; they commence it early in life, and they continue it, until they soon drop into the grave. To use their expression, the way they drink, is 'quite a caution'.

CAPTAIN MARRYAT

Much of this drinking, he found, took place at an institution called a bar:

The bar of an American hotel is generally a very large room on the basement, fitted up very much like our gin palaces in London, not so elegant in its decorations indeed, but on the same system. A long counter runs across it, behind which stand two or three bar-keepers to wait upon the customers, and distribute the various potations, compounded from the contents of several rows of bottles behind them. Here the eye reposes on masses of pure ice

'That at times I drank much more than I wished is certain, yet still I gave most serious offence, especially in the west, because I would not drink early in the morning, or before dinner.'

CAPTAIN MARRYAT

crystal, large bunches of mint, decanters of every sort of wine, every variety of spirits, lemons, sugar, bitters, cigars and tobacco; it really makes one thirsty, even the going into a bar. Here you meet everybody and everybody meets you. Here the Senator, the member of Congress, the merchant, the store-keeper, travellers from the far west and every other part of the country, who have come to purchase goods, all congregate.

Most of them have a cigar in their mouth, some are transacting business, others conversing, some sitting down together whispering confidentially. Here you obtain all the news, all the scandal, all the politics, and all the fun; it is this dangerous propinquity which occasions so much intemperance.

William Fraser Rae, arriving off the train with a group of new acquaintances in Sacramento, described a social custom which he found slightly offensive:

It was proposed that we should 'take a drink.' This proposition was received with general approval. As a stranger, I could neither object with good reason nor retire with courtesy. The 'drink' was duly enjoyed by the several members of the party. Hardly was the libation at an end than the friend of one of those present made his appearance. After a hearty greeting to his friend, the ceremony of introducing those who were strangers to him was performed with the accustomed solemnities. Then followed the invitation, 'Let us take a drink.' Again were healths pledged and glasses emptied at the hotel bar. The gratification was slightly diminished this time, seeing that the night was advancing, and the hour for supper was nigh. But remonstrance was useless, and would have been regarded as unsocial. Under these circumstances cheerful submission is more commendable and wise than flat refusal and unmannerly opposition. But a third and greater trial was on hand. Fresh introductions were made, and new invitations to take a drink were proffered. With as good a grace as I could command, I submitted to an ordeal which was now becoming serious and unpleasant. Happily, the end to the trying and novel welcome had arrived. Each one was now permitted to go his own way and make his own arrangements.

A traveller needed to know what to order at the bar. Henry Bradshaw Fearon noted the popularity of 'eye-openers', 'toddy' and 'phlegm dispensers', while, on an adventurous trip to California in 1860, Sir Richard Francis Burton became familiar with 'tarantula-juice', 'red-eye', 'Jersey lightning', 'leg-stretcher', and 'tangle-leg' (which all turned out to be names for whisky).

While the British were tempted to disapprove of so much drinking at the bar, some also hinted at a certain disappointment on finding no alcohol with their meals: 'it seemed strange to me when I first went to America to drink tea or coffee with every meal; but it is the custom there, and you hardly ever see an American or Canadian drink beer or wine with his dinner,' wrote R. Byron Johnson, an Englishman on a gold-rush trip to British Columbia. And there was another popular drink which British visitors sometimes found even less acceptable than tea and coffee:

> What immoderate water-drinkers the Americans are! there is water in the trains, water in the boats, water in the railway-stations, water in the drawing-rooms, and to make matters worse, at dinner (I am speaking of the table d'hote dinners on the road), instead of taking a little wine or beer, like people in general, they drink oceans of milk diluted with water. It is to me most unpleasant to look at.
>
> CLARA BROMLEY

Ice was also a novelty for the British, who were surprised to learn that it was carefully preserved from the winter, or shipped south in the spring. Charles Weld, walking through Boston at six in the morning, saw a large block dropped at every door; he reported that for four dollars, a household was supplied daily during the five summer months. Sarah Mytton Maury, a well-connected young woman on a tour in 1845, found that 'it is customary when you pay a visit, for the attendant immediately on your arrival to present you with iced water.' Fanny Trollope was impressed with the arrangements in New York: 'I do not imagine that there is a house in the city without the luxury of a piece of ice to cool the water, and harden the butter.' According to Captain Marryat, in hot weather iced water could be more of a hazard than alcohol:

> It is very dangerous to drink iced water, and many have died from yielding to the temptation. One young man came into the bar of the hotel where I resided, drank a glass of water, and fell down dead at the porch.

In Marryat's manly circles, he explained, water, iced or otherwise, was less popular than a trip to the bar: 'as for water, what the man said, when asked to belong to the Temperance Society, appears to be the general opinion: "It's very good for navigation."'

SLEEPING ARRANGEMENTS

Once fed, the weary traveller's priority is a bed – preferably clean, private, and secured without undue argument or confusion. In the nineteenth century, as now, the experienced customer would never settle for what was first offered, as Captain Horton Rhys explained:

> Here a word of advice to all who may follow in my wake, which applies to every Hotel or *House* in every city and town throughout America and Canada. Be you travelling *en garcon*

or *en famille*, on your arrival at an Hotel, walk straight to the *Office*, state the strength of your party, the probably length of your stay, and your requirements, and *make the best bargain you can*. You will then get board and lodging as reasonably as in any country in the world; neglect to do this, and when you peruse your bill at the end of a week, or whenever it may be, if your eyes don't expand beyond their accustomed limits, I am no true historian. They don't add up your score, but pile it, and if you remonstrate, they coolly tell you it is their usual charge *'when no arrangement is made,'* which means they would have done it for half, sooner than you should have applied at another *House*.

The thrifty guest is probably best advised to follow Captain Rhys's assertive tactics. Rudyard Kipling was irritated by the hotel clerks in San Francisco who, with 'swaggering self-consciousness of freedom', gave poor service to the British traveller; when Kipling finally caught the receptionist's attention, he reported, the man would still be 'whistling or humming, or picking his teeth'. Anthony Trollope described the humiliation of hotel check-in procedure, beginning when the guest appeared at the bar, which doubled up as the reception desk:

The guest walks up and there inscribes his name in a book. This inscription was to me a moment of misery which I could never go through with equanimity. As the name is written, and as the request for accommodation is made, half a dozen loungers look over your name and listen to what you say. They listen attentively, and spell your name carefully, but the great man behind the bar does not seem to listen or to heed you. Your destiny is never imparted to you on the instant . . . The great man has listened to my request in silence, with an imperturbable face, and has usually continued his conversation with some loafing friend, who at the time is probably scrutinizing my name in the book. I have often suffered in patience; but patience is not specially the badge of my tribe, and I have sometimes spoken out rather freely. If I may presume to give advice to my travelling countrymen how to act under such circumstances I should recommend to them freedom of speech rather than patience. The great man when freely addressed generally opens his eyes, and selects the key to your room without further delay.

Strangely, somewhat undermining both his own and Rhys's accounts of unreasonable hoteliers, Trollope achieved what Rhys claimed was impossible, a refund without an 'arrangement'. After staying a fortnight at a hotel, he discovered he had been charged a daily rate for his sitting-room instead of a reduced fortnightly rate: 'I felt myself stirred up to complain, and did in that case remonstrate. I was asked how much I wished to have returned, – for the bill had been paid, – and the sum I suggested was at once handed to me.'

In spite of this generous treatment, Trollope was severe on American hotels, and found their

'I do not like the American hotels; but I must say in their favour that they afford an immense amount of accommodation. The traveller is rarely told that an hotel is full, so that travelling in America is without one of those great perils to which it is subject in Europe. It must also be acknowledged that for the ordinary purposes of a traveller they are very cheap.'

ANTHONY TROLLOPE

difficulties in adapting to his required arrangements a continual source of irritation: 'the rule which holds that men at Rome should do as Romans do, if true anywhere, is true in America. Therefore I say that in an American inn one can never do as one pleases.' Here, Trollope was echoing the kind of complaint with which his mother had achieved notoriety in 1832:

Arrived at our inn, a forlorn parlour, filled with the blended fumes of tobacco and whisky, received us; and chilled, as we began to feel ourselves with the mountain air, we preferred going to our cold bedrooms rather than sup in such an atmosphere. We found linen on the beds which they assured us had only been used *a few nights*; every kind of refreshment we asked for we were answered, 'We do not happen to have that article.'

It was with great difficulty that we procured a fire in our bedrooms from the surly-looking *young lady* who condescended to officiate as chambermaid, and with that much more, that we extorted clean linen for our beds; that done, we patiently crept into them supperless, while she made her exit muttering about the difficulty of 'fixing English folks.'

Other writers were more willing to credit the achievements of North American hotels in providing huge numbers of rooms and meals, often with considerable efficiency, even in towns which were only half-built. In particular, the enormous establishments in the big cities were a source of wonder. 'They do things on the most magnificent scale,' wrote Barbara Bodichon from Washington in 1858, 'their hotels are like towns, or rather palaces.' Lady Theodora Guest surveyed her party's rooms in Montreal in 1894, and noted with approval 'the usual bath-rooms, which are so good an addition in all the American hotels, and seem to pervade Canada as well'. And William Fraser Rae, having recorded the frequent first impression of New York, that 'there is nothing strange or foreign to English eyes', withdrew the remark as soon as he entered one of the city's 'monster hotels'. There he found himself 'emphatically an ignorant and bewildered foreigner in an English-speaking land'; he soon learned the system, and concluded enthusiastically that the only foreigners who could possibly grumble at American hotels would be those 'who would stigmatise Paradise as a detestable place of abode if it differed in petty details from the land of their birth'. Americans themselves also appreciated the many and complex demands of the business: William Howard Russell reported that a common expression to describe someone of limited talents was: 'Brown is a clever man, but he can't manage an hotel.'

There was also praise for the way proprietors of smaller hotels and inns treated customers as their personal guests, sitting at the head of the table during meals: Isabella Strange Trotter, on tour with her father in 1858, arrived at the Brevoort House hotel in New York and noted: 'the master of the hotel shook hands with papa on entering, and again this morning treated him with the same republican familiarity.' Captain Marryat enjoyed this personal touch, which he found 'one of the most pleasing features of American society'.

The city hotels, whether large and efficient or small and hospitable, were quite different from the kind of establishments found in country areas. Captain Marryat felt bound to warn his readers of what they might expect if their travels took them to the furthest reaches of organized hospitality:

He who is of the silver-fork school will not find much comfort out of the American cities and large towns. There are no neat, quiet little inns, as in England. It is all the 'rough and tumble' system, and when you stop at humble inns you must expect to eat peas with a two-pronged fork and to sit down to meals with people whose exterior is anything but agreeable, to attend upon yourself, and to sleep in a room in which there are three or four other beds (I have slept in one with nearly twenty), most of them carrying double, even if you do not have a companion in your own.

    A New York friend of mine . . . told me that at a western inn he had particularly requested that he might not have a bed-fellow, and was promised that he should not. On his retiring, he found his bed already occupied, and he went down to the landlady, and expostulated. 'Well,' replied she, 'it's only your *own driver*, I thought you wouldn't mind him.'

The further from 'civilization' the traveller ventured, the greater was the need to make the best of what was offered, as Susanna Moodie discovered when she made her way into the backwoods of Canada for the first time:

> I was tired and hungry, my face disfigured and blistered by the unremitting attentions of the blackflies that rose in swarms from the river. I thought to get a private room to wash and dress in, but there is no such thing as privacy in this country. In the bush, all things are in common; you cannot even get a bed without having to share it with a companion. A bed on the floor in a public sleeping-room! Think of that; a public sleeping-room! – men, women, and children, only divided by a paltry curtain. Oh, ye gods! think of the snoring, squalling, grumbling, puffing; think of the kicking, elbowing, and crowding; the suffocating heat - the mosquitoes, with their infernal buzzing – and you will form some idea of the misery I endured the first night of my arrival in the bush.

Fanny Kemble, travelling through North Carolina on her way to visit her American husband's slave plantations in 1838, was outraged at the suggestion that an elderly aunt of her husband's should share a room with Fanny's maid; the landlord, trying to find beds for everyone, added unhelpfully, as if to lessen the imposition, 'I dare say they have done it a hundred times.'

> This unheard-of proposition, and the man's cool impudence in making it, so astonished me, that I could hardly speak. At last, however, I found words to inform him that none of our party were in the habit of sleeping with each other, and that the arrangement was such as we were not at all inclined to submit. The gentleman, apparently very much surprised at our singular habits, said: 'Oh! he didn't know that the ladies were not acquainted' (as if, forsooth, one went to bed with all one's acquaintance!)

In areas of rapid growth, hotels were the focus of local life, an essential bridge between the tent cities of the frontier and the individual homes of a settled population. Often, for a time,

'The equality of all men is painfully illustrated when your neighbour at table eats with his knife, dips the end of it into the salt, and disregards the object and end of napkins. But it is carried to a more disagreeable extent when it is held to mean that any man who comes to an inn has a right to share your bed.'

WILLIAM HOWARD RUSSELL

demand for accommodation exceeded supply. R. Byron Johnson passed through the booming town of Victoria, British Columbia, in the goldrush of 1861:

> I was not a little surprised, on asking in the conventional manner for a bed for the night, to be shown by the energetic proprietor (in his shirt-sleeves, ready for any emergency) into a billiard room, upon the floor of which he kindly pointed out a space about three feet wide, where I might, in company with forty or fifty others provided with similar accommodation, spread my own blankets, and sleep upon them, for a trifling fee of fifty cents. I remonstrated gently with my host, who appeared somewhat flushed with the prospects of gain held out

by the number of our party, but all the reply I could get was, that 'he reckoned any man that 'ud raise a growl on such an occashin was darned small pertaters.'

Johnson decided this was the best arrangement he could make that night, and settled down, only to be woken by two men who asked general permission to play a game of billiards because a bet of $100 hung on the outcome. The game began, with the players stepping over the drowsy bodies on the floor:

> This arrangement succeeded well enough for some time, till one of the players began to lose the game and his temper, and, heedless for the moment of the position of affairs, brought down the butt-end of his cue on what he fondly imagined was the floor. It happened, however, to be the stomach of a burly young Englishman, who, having the bad taste not to see the joke, jumped up and struck the man with the cue a considerable blow in the eye, knocking him down on the top of a few more of us, including myself. This caused a great row, in which everybody hit out at everybody else; the lights were put out, somebody fired off a pistol, and amidst great confusion the two players somehow got hustled out into the street, there to settle anew, in some other place, their hundred-dollar bet.

CHAPTER THREE

A MANNER OF SPEAKING

In all my travels, both among Heathens and among Christians, I have never encountered any people by whom I found it nearly so difficult to make myself understood as by the Americans.

BASIL HALL

The Americans generally improve upon the inventions of others; probably they may have improved upon our language.

CAPTAIN MARRYAT

Captain Marryat's suggestion is generous, but one cannot help wondering about its sincerity. Basil Hall, on the other hand, is certainly exaggerating but is probably being true to his instincts. British visitors to North America find it almost impossible to avoid assuming a proprietorial attitude to the language they hear. It is, after all, still called English. Countless neologisms and quaint expressions, as they seem to British ears, invite, at the least, some sort of ironic commentary.

For readers unfamiliar with American expressions, a travel writer had to provide translations. In the course of his *Sketches of America*, published in 1818, Henry Bradshaw Fearon offered the following:

English	*American*
Shops	Stores
Timber	Lumber
Tea	Supper
Biscuits	Boston crackers
Negroes	Niggars
Proprietor	Boss

33

Servants	Helps
A load	A jag
Cheating	Shaving
Being ill	Being sick
Gone to bed	Turned in

These were more-or-less direct translations. More interesting were expressions which needed explanation because there was no equivalent in English. Basil Hall was mystified by a word which today seems an unlikely cause of trouble:

> On driving a little beyond the streets towards the woods, we came to a space, about an acre in size, roughly enclosed, on the summit of a gentle swell in the ground.
> 'What can this place be for?'
> 'Oh,' said my companion, 'that is the graveyard.'
> 'Graveyard – what is that?' said I; for I was quite adrift.
> 'Why, surely,' said he, 'you know what a graveyard is? It is a burying ground. All the inhabitants of the place are buried there, whatever be their persuasion. We don't use churchyards in America.'

Likewise, Isabella Strange Trotter recorded:

> If you do not feel very well, and think you are headachy, and that perhaps the weather is the cause, you are told you are 'under the weather this morning.' An excellent expression we think; so truly describing the state papa is often in when in dear old England.

Thomas Hamilton was bemused by a political placard which campaigned with the slogan: 'JACKSON FOR EVER. GO THE WHOLE HOG!':

> I learned, that 'going the whole hog' is the American popular phrase for Radical Reform, and is used by the Democratic party to distinguish them from the Federalists, who are supposed to prefer less sweeping measures, and consequently *to go* only *a part* of the interesting quadruped in question. The *Go-the-whole-hoggers*, therefore, are politicians determined to follow out Democratic principles to their utmost extent, and with this party, General Jackson is at present an especial favourite. The expression, I am told, is of Virginian origin. In that state, when a butcher kills a pig, it is usual to demand of each customer, whether he will 'go the whole hog;' as, by such extensive traffic, a purchaser may supply his table at a lower price, than is demanded of him, whose imagination revels among *prime pieces*, to the exclusion of baser matter.

'The privilege of barbarizing the King's English is assumed by all ranks and conditions of men. Such words as "slick," "kedge," and "boss," it is true, are rarely used by the better orders; but they assume unlimited liberty in the use of "expect," "reckon," "guess," and perpetrate conversational anomalies with the most remorseless impunity.'
THOMAS HAMILTON

Charles Mackay, a journalist who toured America in 1857, devoted a chapter of his *Life and Liberty in America* to language, explaining the following:

To loaf, to idle, or dawdle.
Splurge, a display, an outburst of expenditure.
To make a pile, to make a fortune.
A dough face, a man easily moved to change his opinion.
Bender, a spree.
Whole-souled, a very common phrase in America to express a hearty, enthusiastic person.
Go-a-headitive, progressive, 'fast'.

Travellers acquired the vocabulary for their particular purposes. William Fraser Rae offered a phrase-book for those on the train:

If he would avoid being singular, the English traveller will say 'railroad' instead of railway, 'track' instead of line, 'car' instead of carriage, 'depot,' 'freight-train,' 'baggage-car' instead of station, goods train, and luggage van. Luggage consists of so many 'pieces'; it is not registered but 'checked.' If a portmanteau forms part of it, the portmanteau must be spoken of as a 'valise.' Nor must luggage be asked for, or referred to under any other name than that of 'baggage.'

Rae also gives a full explanation of a word which has almost come to symbolize Americanisms to the British:

The American term 'side-walk' is at once applicable and correct. That part of the street which would be covered with paving-stones in an English city or town is often composed of wooden planking in the towns and cities of America. In the Far West, where wood is often cheaper than stone, wood naturally gets the preference. When the rain does not fall, and where snow is unknown, this wooden pavement is unobjectionable. In Sacramento it is employed under the most favourable conditions.

Captain Marryat, in the first of a series of essays on American institutions published in 1839, tried to equip British visitors with an understanding of American usage. He dealt with a number of potential puzzles:

They are very fond of using the noun as a verb, as —

'I *suspicion* that's a fact.'
'I *opinion* quite the contrary.'

The word *great* is oddly used for fine, splendid.

'She's the *greatest* gal in the whole Union.'

The word *ugly* is used for cross, ill-tempered.

'I did feel so *ugly* when he said that.'

Bad is used in an odd sense: it is employed for awkward, uncomfortable, sorry:

'I did feel so *bad* when I read that' — awkward.

'I have felt quite *bad* about it ever since' – uncomfortable.

'She was so *bad*, I thought she would cry' – sorry.

And bad is tantamount to *not good*. I have heard a lady say:

'I don't feel *at all good* this morning.'

Mean is occasionally used for ashamed.

'I never felt so *mean* in my life.'

The word *handsome* is oddly used.

'We reckon this very *handsome* scenery, sir,' said an American to me, pointing to the landscape.

The Americans are very local in their phrases, and borrow their similes very much from the nature of their occupations and pursuits. If you ask a Virginian or Kentuckian where he was born, he will invariably tell you that he was *raised* in such a county – the term applied to horses, and in breeding states, to men also.

To *make tracks* – to walk away. 'Well, now, I shall *make tracks*'; – from foot-tracks in the snow.

Putting all this together, the reader will be able to translate a passage of full-blooded American, of which Captain Marryat constructed the following specimen:

'Well, he's a pretty substantial man and no mistake. He has got a heart as big as an ox, and everything else in proportion, I've a notion. He loves Sal, the worst kind . . . aren't she a screamer? I were thinking of Sal myself, for I feel lonesome, and when I am thrown into my store promiscuous alone, I can tell you I have the blues, the worst kind, no mistake – I can tell you that. I always feel a kind o' queer when I sees Sal, but when I meet any of the other gals I am as calm and cool as the milky way.'

Finally, there was an important piece of non-verbal communication, whose usefulness Captain Marryat readily admitted:

There are two syllables – *um, hu* – which are very generally used by the Americans as a sort of reply, intimating that they are attentive and that the party may proceed with his narrative; but, by inflection and intonation, these two syllables are made to express dissent or assent,

'The Americans dwell upon their words when they speak — a custom arising, I presume, from their cautious, calculating habits; and they have always more or less of a nasal twang.'

CAPTAIN MARRYAT

surprise, disdain, and . . . a great deal more. The reason why these two syllables have been selected is that they can be pronounced without the trouble of opening your mouth, and you may be in a state of listlessness and repose while others talk. I myself found them very convenient at times, and gradually got into the habit of using them.

None of this advice would usually allow a British traveller to pass for an American, because of the difference in accent: Rudyard Kipling reported that he was 'pitied' for speaking with an English accent, and Charles Dickens described how his wife was expected to be pleased when her accent was not recognized:

A St. Louis lady complimented Kate upon her voice and manner of speaking, assuring her that she should never have suspected her of being Scotch, or even English. She was so obliging as to add that she would have taken her for an American, anywhere; which she (Kate) was no doubt aware was a very great compliment, as the Americans were admitted on all hands to have greatly refined upon the English language!

For those unfamiliar with an American accent, Charles Mackay offered the following examples of what he called 'mispronunciations':

. . . 'ben' for 'been', 'air' for 'are', 'ant-*eye*-slavery' for 'anti-slavery', 'Eye-taly' for 'Italy', 'Eye-talian' for 'Italian', 'dye-plomatic' for 'diplomatic', and invariably '*my*self' for the more subdued mode in which we in the 'old country' pronounce these two egotistical syllables.

While Dickens noted that 'out of Boston and New York a nasal drawl is universal', William Fraser Rae attempted some finer regional distinctions: 'in New England the voice is sharp and shrill; in the South slow and liquid; in the West deep-toned and resonant'. Thomas Hamilton was content to generalize, describing the American accent as 'a peculiar modulation, partaking of a snivel and a drawl, which, I confess, to my ear, is no means laudable on the score of euphony'. Hamilton was unimpressed with American use of language: they were 'babarizing the King's English', and had 'chosen arbitrarily to change the meaning of certain old and established English words, for reasons which they cannot explain'. Their use of the word 'clever' was a typical example:

A good-natured blockhead in the American vernacular, is a clever man, and having had this drilled into me, I foolishly imagined that all trouble with regard to this word at least, was at an end. It was not long, however, before I heard of a gentleman having moved into a *clever* house, of another succeeding to a *clever* sum of money, of a third embarking in a *clever* ship, and making a *clever* voyage, with a *clever* cargo; and of the sense attached to the word in these combinations, I could gain nothing like satisfactory explanation.

By his own account, Hamilton made a complete nuisance of himself with his pedantry, refusing to admit, for example that 'a very plain, but agreeable lady' was '*a very fine woman*', because, to him, *fine* referred to a person's physical features: 'I therefore ventured to hint, that the personal charms of Mrs —— were certainly not her principal attraction, but that I had rarely enjoyed the good fortune of meeting a lady more pleasing and intelligent.' By the end of this awkward exchange, Hamilton has learnt that 'in the dialect of this country, the term *fine woman* refers exclusively to the intellect'.

No doubt there were countless other examples of British visitors querying Americans on their language with a self-righteous authority. But not all British visitors were as dogmatic: Oscar Wilde, who enjoyed a successful lecture tour of the States and Canada in 1881, characteristically argued against conventional wisdom, claiming that 'what many people call Americanisms are really old English expressions which have lingered in our colonies while they have been lost in our own country.' He gave as an example the expression 'I guess', which he found used in the American sense by the seventeenth-century English philosopher John Locke, in his *Essay on Human Understanding*.

Another endless source of entertainment for British visitors was the selection of place-names in North America. The critic Matthew Arnold, who undertook two lecture tours in the 1880s, summed up the British attitude when he referred to 'the jumble of unnatural and inappropriate names everywhere'. Others expounded this view:

On first looking at the map, and more particularly on hearing stage-drivers, talking of Troy, Ithaca, and Rome, and still more when I heard them speaking of the towns of Cicero, Homer or Manlius, an involuntary smile found its way to the lips, followed often by a good hearty laugh. The oddity and incongruity of the thing were much heightened by the admixture of such modern appelations as Truxton, Sullivan, and Tompkins, jumbled up with the Indian names of Onodaga, Oneida, and Chitteningo.

BASIL HALL

Frances Wright was a young Scottish woman who toured America with her sister in 1818, later publishing an unfashionably enthusiastic account of her experiences. On this subject, even she had reservations:

There is, it must be confessed, the strangest confusion of names in the western counties of this state that ingenuity could well imagine. In one district you have all the poets from Homer and Pope, nay, for aught I know, they may come down to Byron; in another, you have a collection of Roman heroes; in a third, all the mighty cities of the world, from the great Assyrian empire downwards; and, scattered among this classic confusion, relics of the Indian vocabulary, which, I must observe, are often not the least elegant and are indisputably always the most appropriate.

FRANCES WRIGHT

The British were unanimous in approving the use of Indian names, which Captain Marryat said the Americans should not feel guilty about borrowing: after all, he wrote, 'they have robbed the Indians of everything else'. Marryat conducted a comprehensive survey of American place-names, which revealed that many were inspired by people, the most popular

The Writers

ROBERT LOUIS STEVENSON (1850–94) went to California in 1879, against the wishes of his parents, to marry Fanny Osbourne, an American woman he had met in France. He was short of money, and travelled steerage, a journey he recorded in *The Amateur Emigrant* (1895). While Mrs Osbourne was waiting for a divorce, Stevenson lived in San Francisco, visiting her when he could. Their honeymoon in nearby Calistoga later appeared as *The Silverado Squatters* (1883). The couple returned to Europe, where *Treasure Island* (1882) made Stevenson's name. They revisited San Francisco at the start of a long voyage in the South Seas, where Stevenson died at the home they bought in Samoa. On his first visit to the States, Stevenson was twenty-nine. He recorded his feelings about its attraction to the youth of Britain: 'it will be hard for an American to understand the spirit. But let him imagine a young man, who shall have grown up in an old and rigid circle, following bygone fashions and taught to distrust his own fresh instincts, and who now suddenly hears of a family of cousins, all about his own age, who keep house together by themselves and live far from restraint and tradition; let him imagine this, and he will have some imperfect notion of the sentiment with which spirited English youths turn to the thought of the American Republic.'

being Washington (43 places), Jackson (41) and Jefferson (32); of other towns and villages, there were 33 Blacks, 15 Whites and 10 Yellows, 23 Beavers, 21 Buffaloes, 11 Racoons, 25 Cedars, 15 Swans and 1 Bear's Rump.

Robert Louis Stevenson, embracing the incongruities, offered a rare eulogy to American names:

> There is no part of the world in which nomenclature is so rich, poetical, humorous, and picturesque as the United States of America. All times, races, and languages have brought their contribution. Pekin is in the same state with Euclid, with Bellefontaine, and with Sandusky. Chelsea, with its London associations of red brick, Sloane Square, and the King's Road, is own suburb to stately and primeval Memphis . . . Old, red Manhattan lies, like an Indian arrow-head under a steam factory, below Anglified New York. The names of the States and Territories themselves form a chorus of sweet and most romantic vocables: Delaware, Ohio, Indiana, Florida, Dakota, Iowa, Wyoming, Minnesota, and the Carolinas; there are few poems with a nobler music for the ear: a songful, tuneful land; and if the new Homer shall arise from the Western continent, his verse will be enriched, his pages sing spontaneously, with the names of states and cities that would strike the fancy in a business circular.

To many British writers, the idea of an American Homer would have been laughable; indeed, to some, the prospects for ordinary communication in English looked bleak. Thomas Hamilton predicted that by the end of the twentieth century Britain and America would no longer be able to communicate:

> I will not go on with this unpleasant subject; nor should I have alluded to it, but that I feel it something of a duty to express the natural feeling of an Englishman, at finding the language of Shakespeare and Milton thus gratuitously degraded. Unless the present progress of change be arrested, by an increase of taste and judgment in the more educated classes, there can be no doubt that, in another century, the dialect of the Americans will become utterly unintelligible to an Englishman, and that the nation will be cut off from the advantages arising from their participation in British literature. If they contemplate such an event with complacency, let them go on and prosper; they have only to '*progress*' in their present course, and their grandchildren bid fair to speak a jargon as novel and peculiar as the most patriotic American linguist can desire.

CHAPTER FOUR

ON THE ROAD

It seems that everybody travels in America, and that nothing is thought of distance.

ANTHONY TROLLOPE

British visitors who imagined themselves providing at least a minor point of interest to their North American hosts on account of their long journey 'to see the lions', as tourism was known, were surprised to discover that their itinerary – much more ambitious than anything possible in Britain – was quite unremarkable on a continent where people seemed to spend their whole lives in transit.

A young man will step into a car and sit beside you, with that easy, careless air which is common to a railway passenger in England who is passing from one station to the next; and on conversing with him you will find that he is going seven or eight hundred miles. He is supplied with fresh newspapers three or four times a day as he passes by the towns at which they are published; he eats a large assortment of gum-drops and apples, and is quite as much at home as in his own house. On board the river boat it is the same with him, with this exception, that when there he can get whisky when he wants it. He knows nothing of the ennui of travelling, and never seems to long for the end of his journey, as travellers do with us. Should his boat come to grief upon the river, and lie by for a day or night, it does not in the least disconcert him. He seats himself upon three chairs, takes a bite of tobacco, thrusts his hands into his trousers pockets and revels in an elysium of his own.

ANTHONY TROLLOPE

George Borrett, on tour in Canada in 1864, found attitudes there the same:

One old gentleman told me that he took his family to the seaside, 1800 miles, every year, and 1800 back, with less trouble and concern, I dare say, than a Londoner would make about going down to Ipswich. A youth of fifteen thinks himself ill-used, if he has not seen all the great cities of his country and the interior of every state . . . So the nation is in a chronic state of 'fidgets.' Men and women of every age, babies in arms, and men who are called old, females almost as numerous as the males, crowd the cars, stuff the steamboats, overwhelm the omnibuses, and storm the hotels.

Trans-continental rail lines made the longest journeys, in theory, simply a matter of sitting on a train and waiting to arrive. William Fraser Rae, on his way from New York to San Francisco in 1869, wrote of the Pacific Railway being responsible for 'the comparative annihilation of ideas as to distance in the minds of those who travel by it'. Captain Marryat commented:

Time to an American is everything, and space he attempts to reduce to a mere nothing . . . The mania for travelling, among the people of the United States, renders it most important that everything connected with locomotion should be well arranged; society demands it, public opinion enforces it, and therefore, with few exceptions, it is so.

Marryat's confidence was seldom echoed in other writers' accounts; and Marryat himself admitted that for all its efficiency, American travel was hazardous:

At present, it certainly is more dangerous to travel one week in America than to cross the Atlantic a dozen times. The number of lives lost in one year by accidents in steamboats, railroads, and coaches was estimated, in a periodical which I read in America, at *one thousand seven hundred and fifty*!

Although often worried about their safety, British writers on all forms of American transport were preoccupied with questions of comfort. Whether they travelled by road, rail or river, there was plenty to get used to, and, once in a while, something to admire.

OVERLAND

Much as I had seen and heard of the badness of the roads in Canada, I was not prepared for such a one as we travelled along this day: indeed, it hardly deserved the name of a road, being little more than an opening hewed out through the woods, the trees being felled and drawn aside so as to admit a wheeled carriage passing along.

The swamps and little forest streams, that occasionally gush across the path, are rendered passable by logs placed side by side. From the ridgy and striped appearance of these bridges they are aptly enough termed corduroy.

Over these abominable corduroys the vehicle jolts, jumping from log to log, with a shock that must be endured with as good grace as possible. If you could bear these knocks, and pitiless thumpings and bumpings, without wry faces, your patience and philosophy would far exceed mine; sometimes I laughed because I would not cry.

CATHERINE PARR TRAILL

'When we halted to change horses (the driver) told the outside passengers to hold on firmly, as he meant "to go ahead like greased lightning." As the road before us looked even worse than that behind, this intimation seemed equivalent to a threat of extra sufferings about to be inflicted. On the other hand, the warning was accepted with gratitude. It was better to have one's misery shortened in time, even if intensified in degree.'

WILLIAM FRASER RAE

Mrs Traill was driving with her husband to their newly-purchased land in the backwoods of Ontario. Charles Dickens also suffered a corduroy road, on his way from Columbus, Ohio, north to Lake Erie:

> The very slightest of jolts with which the ponderous carriage fell from log to log, was enough, it seemed, to have dislocated all the bones in the human body. It would be impossible to experience a similar set of sensations, in any other circumstances, unless perhaps in attempting to go up to the top of St Paul's in an omnibus. Never, never once, that day, was the coach in any position, attitude, or kind of motion to which we are accustomed in coaches. Never did it make the smallest approach to one's experience of the proceedings of any sort of vehicle that goes on wheels.

Even on the relatively busy New England route from Providence to Boston, Thomas Hamilton found himself on a road of 'deep ruts, and huge stones', which he noted at the time as being the worst in the world, 'an opinion, which my subsequent experience as a traveller in the United States, has long since induced me to retract':

English readers may smile when one talks seriously of the punishment of being jolted in a stage-coach, but to arrive at the end of a journey with bruised flesh and aching bones, is, on the whole, not particularly pleasant . . . On the present occasion, to say nothing of lateral concussion, twenty times at least was I pitched up with violence against the roof of the coach, which, being as ill provided with stuffing as the cushions below, occasioned a few changes in my phrenological developments. One of the passengers, however, – a grave valetudinarian – assured me, that such unpleasant exercise was an admirable cure for dyspepsy, and that when suffering under its attacks, he found an unfailing remedy in being jolted over some forty or fifty miles of such roads as that we now travelled. At the moment, I certainly felt more inclined to pity him for the remedy than the disease.

While bruises and bumps were a standard accompaniment of travel on North American roads, more serious danger was possible when passengers found themselves in the hands of a casually reckless driver. Charles Weld hired a buggy driven by a silent, spitting young man in Cincinnati to run an errand, ironically, the inspection of a tomb in the city's cemetary:

I am not a nervous man, so, although we went at a break-neck rate, careering over stones and through deep ruts, I made no remonstrance, having faith in the springs. But when, on turning a corner, we came suddenly in sight of a board, with the well-known notice, '*Look out for the locomotive when the bell rings*,' which was made more impressive by hearing the signal, and seeing the line of steam announcing the proximity of a train, I was somewhat anxious, as my driver did not manifest the slightest disposition to stop. As usual, the road and railway crossed on the same level, which did not lessen my anxiety. 'Hold hard! stop, stop!' I cried; and as these words received no attention, I rose from my seat and grasped the driver's arm, for the purpose of arresting our progress; but in vain. Lashing the horse with redoubled energy, he replied to my entreaties to stop, by the assurance he would go a-head of the en-*gine*; and to my horror, on we went, buggy and train approximating rapidly at right angles; the locomotive's bell meanwhile ringing furiously what seemed to be my death knell. Finding all my efforts to avert an anticipated collision were futile, I resumed my seat, and resigned myself to my fate. What I did or said during the next few moments I know not; but I remember a feeling of sickness came over me as we dashed across the line, and I beheld the iron horse rushing onwards, and almost felt the hot blast of its steam-jets.

'There, I told you I'd clear the darn'd thing,' said my driver, chuckling over the achievement; 'but 'twas a close shave.'

'The most general, the most rapid, the most agreeable, and, at the same time, the most dangerous of American travelling is by steamboats.'

CAPTAIN MARRYAT

OVER WATER

The steamboat allowed the traveller to nurse the bruises and calm the nerves after the stage-coach, and, at its best, offered good food and accommodation. It also presented an entertaining tableau of local society, as George Borrett found on his way from Quebec to Montreal:

> The American river-boat, of which the Canadian is a copy, is nothing more nor less than an immense floating hotel, a characteristic type of the people themselves, a curious combination of democratic follies and aristocratic propensities; a mixture of every kind of life – fast life, slow life, busy life, and lazy life, all under one roof. The saloon is a fine handsome room of great length and good height, fitted up with exaggerated decorations, extravagant and, as I think, tasteless. Along either side are the state cabins, each and all a

good bedroom in itself, comfortably arranged and well-ventilated; and around them, on the outside, runs a sort of open deck or platform, where the passengers sit and promenade at their pleasure. At 6 p.m. was served in the saloon, at the lower end, which is set apart as a dining-room, a handsome 'high tea;' and after tea there was music, cards, chess, and so on, till late in the evening, when, after a final moonlight walk outside, the passengers turned in.

I know (at *present*, at least) no other place where you can see a working artisan in fustian sitting down at table next a well-dressed lady, and lounging on an elegant sofa side by side with a high-bred swell.

This physically and politically comfortable mode of transport was not always as popular. When the temperate air of the St Lawrence was replaced by the heat of the Ohio, a traveller could become decidedly tetchy:

I have often heard the expression 'Hell afloat' applied to very uncomfortable ships in the service, but this metaphor ought to have been reserved for a small high-pressure steamboat in the summer months in America; the sun darting his fierce rays down upon the roof above you, which is only half-inch plank, and rendering it so hot that you quickly remove your hand if, by chance, you put it there; the deck beneath your feet so heated by the furnaces below that you cannot walk with slippers; you are panting and exhausted between these two fires, without a breath of air to cool your forehead. Go forward, and the chimneys radiate a heat which is even more intolerable. Go – but there is nowhere to go, except overboard, and then you lose your passage. It is, really, a fiery furnace, and, day or night it is vain to seek a cool retreat.

CAPTAIN MARRYAT

Unfortunately, the steamboat could be dangerous as well as uncomfortable. Its engine was the home of the now metaphorical 'safety valve', a device designed to prevent an explosion when the engines were under too much pressure. But the system didn't always work. Like a nervous passenger in a modern airline, the steamboat traveller was offered luxury and entertainment while worrying privately about imminent disaster. Edward Sullivan catalogued the grim details:

During a fortnight's residence at Niagara, one Yankee steamer was blown up on Lake Erie, with a hundred and fifty passengers; every soul lost but two, who escaped by diving under the sinking mass of passengers, (who stuck to each other like frog-spawn,) and swimming half a mile to shore. One of the two had lost mother, wife, and five children, so had to begin life quite afresh. Another steamer burst her boiler, killing eight outright; other ten were drowned, and thirty were boiled, scalded, and skinned, in such a way they were not expected to survive. Another steamer ran on a rock in Niagara River, and sank in twenty feet of water; her passengers were saved by another steamer.

Sullivan's outspoken account of his tour of both North and South America in 1850, *Rambles and Scrambles*, revealed a taste for danger; but more level-headed travellers were also nervous of steamboats. Charles Dickens survived them without incident, but was aware of his luck:

> We had, for ourselves, a tiny state-room with two berths in it, opening out of the ladies' cabin. There was, undoubtedly, something satisfactory in this 'location,' inasmuch as it was in the stern, and we had been a great many times very gravely recommended to keep as far aft as possible, 'because the steamboats generally blew up forward.' Nor was this an unnecessary caution, as the occurrence and circumstances of more than one such fatality during our stay sufficiently testified.
>
> Passing one of these boats at night, and seeing the great body of fire . . . that rages and roars beneath the frail pile of painted wood: the machinery, not warded off or guarded in any way, but doing its work in the midst of the crowd of idlers and emigrants and children, who throng the lower deck: under the management, too, of reckless men whose acquaintance with its mysteries may have been of six months' standing: one feels directly that the wonder is, not that there should be so many fatal accidents, but that any journey should be safely made.

THE RAILROAD

> We were running across the continent on a bee-line, and I sat for an hour on the rear platform of the rear car to enjoy the wonderful beauty of the sunset and the atmosphere. Far as one could see in the crystalline air there was nothing but desert. The jagged Humboldt ranges flaming in the sunset, with snow in their clefts, though forty-five miles off, looked within an easy canter. The bright metal track, purpling like all else in the cool distance, was all that linked one with eastern or western civilisation.
>
> ISABELLA BIRD

Bird's journey, travelling alone through the Rockies in 1873, demanded enormous strength and perseverance. She was at her most impressive fighting snow and storms on a small horse in the mountains, but she still appreciated the comforts of a train. Crossing the deserts of Utah and Nevada, she had picked up the train the night before, near Lake Tahoe in California. She stepped from the rough western town of Truckee ('fires blazing out of doors, lights glaring, gaming-tables thronged, fiddle and banjo in frightful discord, and the air ringing with ribaldry and profanity') into a world cut off from reality, which provided its passengers with a potent link between places far apart along the 'bright metal track':

'The train calls at stations in the woods, where the wild impossibility of anybody having the smallest reason to get out, is only to be equalled by the apparently desperate hopelessness of there being anybody to get in.'
CHARLES DICKENS

On presenting my ticket at the double door of a 'Silver Palace' car, the slippered steward, whispering low, conducted me to my berth – a luxurious bed three and a half feet wide, with a hair mattress on springs, fine linen sheets, and costly California blankets. The twenty-four inmates of the car were all invisible, asleep behind rich curtains. It was a true temple of Morpheus. Profound sleep was the object to which everything was dedicated. Four silver lamps hanging from the roof, and burning low, gave a dreamy light. On each side of the centre passage, rich rep curtains, green and crimson, striped with gold, hung from silver bars running near the roof, and trailed on the soft Axminster carpet.

Bird was a tough traveller, and this was an exceptionally luxurious sleeper, for which passengers paid extra. In most British reports, the facilities of the train fell short of expectations. The American locomotive, burning wood instead of coal, made a different noise from those back home ('comparable only to the simultaneous braying of a dozen donkeys labouring under oppressive asthma,' said Charles Weld). The engine's emissions were a frequent cause for complaint: the atmosphere in the carriage would be too hot with the windows closed; but when they were opened, flying cinders would set fire to the passengers' clothes:

> The locomotive was of great power, and as it snorted along with a train of carriages of half a mile long in tow, it threw out such showers of fire that we were constantly in danger of conflagration . . . The ladies, assisted by the gentlemen, were constantly employed in putting out the sparks which settled on their clothes.
>
> CAPTAIN MARRYAT

> The ashes and cinders from the engine blew in upon us in showers, penetrating every nook and corner, and certainly neither contributing to our comfort nor cleanliness. We looked like a set of sweeps before reaching our journey's end.
>
> CLARA BROMLEY

The engine was an even greater danger to the cattle wandering across the track, but was itself protected from them by a special device fixed to its front:

> The locomotive is very unlike ours, being an uncouth-looking machine, with a prodigious bottle-nose chimney, and an iron-barred vizor-like affair in front, called a cow-catcher, though, as I can attest from observation, it is not at all particular as to the kind of animal it catches, or kills; for, as may be imagined, when an unfortunate beast is struck by the pointed guard, the chances are it is killed. As the railways, with few exceptions, are unprovided with fences, the herds and flocks turned into the forests are at liberty to roam on the track; sheep especially are fond of resorting to the line at night, which they find drier than the damp clearings. These animals, however, are not deemed formidable obstacles. An engine cleverly dashed through a flock of one hundred and eighty, the greater portion of which were summarily converted into mutton.
>
> CHARLES WELD

William Fraser Rae's train from Salt Lake City to Reno was derailed when it hit a couple of oxen. It was early morning, and the passengers were woken with a start. Rae was impressed to see that some of them were soon out beside the track lighting a fire of sage brush and carving ox steaks with their pen-knives to cook for breakfast.

There were also more conventional sources of provisions on board the train:

We made various purchases as we went along. First came the ticket man, then cheap periodicals, then apples and pears, common bon-bons, and corn pop, of which I am trying to keep a specimen to send you. It is a kind of corn which is roasted on the fire, and in so doing makes a *popping* noise, whence its name. It is pleasant to nibble. Then came iced water, highly necessary after the dry corn pop, and finally about twenty good and well-chosen books. Papa bought the Life of Stephenson.

ISABELLA STRANGE TROTTER

Chief among these providers of services on the train was the conductor, who held an awesome power over the passengers' happiness. The young, impoverished Robert Louis Stevenson, having rowed with his parents in Edinburgh and decided to join his lover in San Francisco in 1879, travelled in the discomfort of an emigrant train. He and his fellow passengers were treated with contempt by the conductor, who would not even bother to shout 'All aboard' before the train was leaving a station. Thus every snatched meal turned into a trial of nerves and speed: 'the train stole from the station without note of warning, and you had to keep an eye upon it even while you ate'. Stevenson recorded other forms of disrespect:

I asked a conductor one day at what time the train would stop for dinner; as he made no answer I repeated the question, with a like result; a third time I returned to the charge, and then Jack-in-office looked me coolly in the face for several seconds and turned ostentatiously away. I believe he was half-ashamed of his brutality; for when another person made the same inquiry, although he still refused the information, he condescended to answer, and even to justify his reticence in a voice loud enough for me to hear. It was, he said, his principle not to tell people where they were to dine; for one answer led to many other questions, as what o'clock it was? or, how soon should we be there? and he could not afford to be eternally worried.

The best hope for information, and a little conversation, according to Charles Dickens, came from one's fellow-passengers:

Everybody talks to you, or to anybody else who hits his fancy. If you are an Englishman, he expects that that railroad is pretty much like an English railroad. If you say 'No,' he says 'Yes?' (interrogatively), and asks in what respect they differ. You enumerate the heads of difference, one by one, and he says 'Yes?' (still interrogatively) to each. Then he guesses that you don't travel faster in England; and on your replying that you do, says, 'Yes?' again (still interrogatively), and, it is quite evident, don't believe it. After a long pause he remarks,

'Yesterday had been a great day for track-laying. The contractor had made arrangements for endeavouring to lay more rails in one day than had ever been done on any American line; and they had looked forward to laying ten miles in one working day.'

W. HENRY BARNEBY, NEAR CALGARY, ALBERTA, 1883

partly to you, and partly to the knob on the top of his stick, that 'Yankees are reckoned to be considerable of a go-ahead people too;' upon which you say 'Yes,' and then he says 'Yes' again (affirmatively this time); and upon your looking out of window, tells you that behind that hill, and some three miles from the next station, there is a clever town in a smart lo-ca-tion, where he expects you have con-cluded to stop. Your answer in the negative naturally leads to more questions in reference to your intended route (always pronounced rout); and wherever you are going, you invariably learn that you can't get there without immense difficulty and danger, and that all the great sights are somewhere else.

For all its deficiencies, the American railroad was a remarkable endeavour; the sheer size of the network, the ability to transport people and goods through the steepest mountain ranges, and the opportunities it offered for trade, were all inspiring achievements. Stevenson had the toughest train journey across country, poor, crowded in, and sick, but he still recognized the grandeur of the enterprise, and its cost:

When I think how the railroad has been pushed through the unwatered wilderness and haunt of savage tribes, and now will bear an emigrant for some twelve pounds from the Atlantic to the Golden Gates; how at each stage of the construction, roaring, impromptu cities, full of gold and lust and death, sprang up and then died away again, and are now but wayside stations in the desert; how in these uncouth places pig-tailed Chinese pirates worked side by side with border ruffians and broken men from Europe, talking together in a mixed dialect, mostly oaths, drinking, quarrelling and murdering like wolves; how the plumed hereditary lord of all America heard, in this last fastness, the scream of the 'bad medicine-waggon' charioting his foes; and then when I go on to remember that all this epical turmoil was conducted by gentlemen in frock-coats, and with a view to nothing more extraordinary than a fortune and a subsequent visit to Paris, it seems to me, I own, as if this railway were the one typical achievement of the age in which we live.

CHAPTER FIVE

NEW SOCIETIES

Even British visitors who were disappointed with the familiarity of some of what they found in North America soon came to recognize that life was also unexpectedly different in rather fundamental ways. From birth to death, social customs and practices were based on assumptions which were seldom articulated, but whose effects were obvious, and sometimes upsetting to British eyes.

It began in the nursery, where, by British standards, children were over-indulged, as Susanna Moodie reported from Canada:

Large parties given to very young children, which are so common in this country, are very pernicious in the way in which they generally operate upon youthful minds. They foster the passions of vanity and envy, and produce a love of dress and display which is very repulsive in the character of a child.

Others came to the same conclusion. Fanny Kemble, an English actress who married an American, had difficulty preventing her daughter being treated like American children. She found the child faced a continuous danger wherever she went:

I allude to the ignorant and fatal practice of the women of stuffing their children from morning till night with every species of trash which comes to hand . . . It becomes a matter of no little difficulty to enforce my own rigid discipline in the midst of the various offers of dainties which tempt my poor little girl at every turn; but I persevere, nevertheless, and am not seldom rewarded by the admiration which her appearance of health and strength excites wherever she goes.

British travellers without children of their own to protect were just as critical of what they saw as the indulgence of American children. Barbara Bodichon, a writer and painter, touring the slave states in 1857, witnessed the following scene in a hotel restaurant in Mobile, Alabama:

'From its earliest years, every American child spends most of its time in correcting the faults of its father and mother.'
OSCAR WILDE

There were two little children *alone*, one not more than two, the other four. The littlest (for the other was little) could not reach the plate with her chin, yet she ordered without hesitation three different meats and tea with all the aplomb of a woman. The negress waiter asked the children what they would have just as if they were grown up! The children here are detestable.

Anthony Trollope hinted that this failure to curb natural but undesirable appetites in children would lead to political problems in the future:

Care-laden mothers would tuck the bibs under the chins of their tyrant children, and some embryo senator of four years old would listen with concentrated attention, while the negro servant recapitulated to him the delicacies of the supper-table, in order that he might make his choice with due consideration. 'Beef-steak,' the embryo four-year old senator would lisp, 'and stewed potato, and buttered toast, and corn cake, and coffee, – and-and-and-; mother, mind you get me the pickles.'

Trollope noted that children were never punished or disciplined, yet he described them as 'an unhappy race . . . my heart has bled for them'. Captain Marryat witnessed a three-year-old boy defying his father's instructions; the father then turned to Marryat and praised the boy for being 'a sturdy republican'. Oscar Wilde noted that in America 'the young are always ready to give to those who are older than themselves the full benefits of their inexperience'. And on the rare occasions when society intervened in relations between old and young, in British eyes it only made things worse. Fanny Trollope commented on a law in Ohio which allowed fathers to be fined for hitting children: 'such a law, they say, generates a spirit of freedom. What else may it generate?'

In other areas of life, where British society would have demanded a certain discipline, American was without conventions. There was, for instance, a disturbing nonchalance in relation to death: 'I do not think the Americans think so much of death as we do,' remarked Barbara Bodichon, after witnessing the coldly efficient arrangements which followed a passenger's death on a steamer. After a show of sympathy for the widow, kindly ladies on board were 'laughing just as merrily the next half hour though they were dressing the body in the cabin'. Lady Theodora Guest discussed cable cars with a resident of Pittsburgh: 'I observed how dangerous the cars seemed, but he said there was no real danger in them: "None at all, though they do kill a good many children."' Other writers reported the same casual attitudes:

> I witnessed, during my short stay here, that indifference to the destruction of life, so very remarkable in this country. The rail-car crushed the head of a child of about seven years old, as it was going into the engine-house; the other children ran to the father, a blacksmith, who was at work at his forge close by, crying out: 'Father, Billy killed.' The man put down his hammer, walked leisurely to where the boy lay, in a pool of his own blood, took up the body, and returned with it under his arm to his house, In a short time, the hammer rang upon the anvil as before.
>
> CAPTAIN MARRYAT

Isabella Bird found herself staying at an inn at Colorado Springs, along with a sick young man whose bedroom door opened on to the main parlour:

> The seven or eight people in the room in which I was were talking, laughing, and playing backgammon, and none laughed louder than the landlady, who was sitting where she saw that mysterious door as plainly as I did. All this time, and during the movings in the room, I saw two large white feet sticking up at the end of the bed. I watched and watched, hoping those feet would move, but they did not; and somehow, to my thinking, they grew stiffer and whiter, and then my horrible suspicion deepened, that while we were sitting there a human spirit untended and desolate had passed forth into the night . . . And still the

THE WRITERS

ISABELLA BIRD (1831–1904) was the frail daughter of an English clergyman who became one of the most extraordinary travellers of the nineteenth century. When she was twenty-three, her doctor recommended a long trip, and she set off on her first expedition to Canada and the United States in 1854, which she recounted as *The Englishwoman in America* (1856). She returned home, her father died, and for more than a decade she lived with her mother and sister, before leaving for Australia, Hawaii, and the Rockies. The last part of this route was recorded in *A Lady's Life in the Rocky Mountains* (1879), which established Bird as a celebrated and best-selling writer. Subsequent journeys took her to Japan and Malaya. She married a quiet, kindly doctor, prompting a joke that she had decided to cancel a trip to New Guinea because it wasn't the sort of place you could take a man to. Five years later, approaching her sixties, Bird found herself a widow, and set off to Tibet, Korea, China and Morocco. After all the dangers and deprivations of her travels, she died peacefully in bed in Edinburgh. Her casual hardiness in the Rockies was evident from her account of a stormy night in a mountain hut: 'I had gone to sleep with six blankets on, and a heavy sheet over my face. Between two and three I was awoke by the cabin being shifted from underneath by the wind, and the sheet was frozen to my lips. I put out my hands, and the bed was thickly covered with fine snow. Getting up to investigate matters, I found the floor some inches deep in parts in fine snow, and a gust of fine, needle-like snow stung my face. The bucket of water was solid ice. I lay in bed freezing till sunrise, when some of the men came to see if I "was alive," and to dig me out.'

landlady laughed and talked, and afterwards said to me, 'It turns the house upside down when they just come here and die.'

Charles Weld illustrated what he described as the 'extraordinary disregard of human life' with a story, 'which we must hope is truthful only in its moral':

'Jack,' said a man to a lad just entering his teens, 'your father's drowned.' 'Darn it,' replied the young hopeful; 'and he's got my knife in his pocket.'

This lack of concern for form in public behaviour extended to the law-courts, where Britain's pomp and ceremony were replaced with a more relaxed American model. Thomas Hamilton visited the Supreme Court of New York state in 1830:

A jury, which had previously retired to deliberate, came into court, and proceeded in the usual form to deliver their verdict. It was not without astonishment, I confess, that I remarked that three-fourths of the jurymen were engaged in eating bread and cheese, and that the foreman actually announced the verdict with his mouth full, ejecting the disjointed syllables during the intervals of mastication! In truth, an American seems to look on a judge, exactly as he does on a carpenter or coppersmith, and it never occurs to him, that an administrator of justice is entitled to greater respect than a constructor of brass knockers, or the sheather of a ship's bottom.

It would be too easy to claim that Americans' lack of respect for authority extended all the way up to the Almighty; in fact, Anthony Trollope found the States, as a nation, 'prone to acknowledge the goodness of God in all things'. But certainly, many of the same forces which influenced secular affairs were seen at work in religious matters. There was no guidance from the state to recommend a particular faith, and British visitors were surprised by the large number of churches competing for congregations, and the complete harmony with which they co-existed. Henry Bradshaw Fearon made a survey in Philadelphia:

The sects of this city, and the number of their places of assembly, are as follow: 1 Swedish Lutheran, 3 Quakers, 1 Free ditto, or Whig Quakers, called also Fighting Quakers, 4 Episcopalian, 4 Baptist, 5 Presbyterian, 4 Roman Catholic, 6 German Lutheran, 1 Moravian, 1 Covenanters, 3 Methodists, 1 Universalist, 1 Unitarian, 1 Independent, 1 Jew, 2 Black Methodist, and 1 Black Episcopalian.

Religious controversy appears unknown. Every man is expected to choose one of these churches; and when that is done, he must abide by it as solemnly and as regularly as he does his cigar, his rum, and his business.

Rebecca Burland, settling in Illinois, did not welcome the free choice she was offered between denominations:

> How far a person's private judgment ought to be at liberty to originate, select, or improve modes of faith and worship, I pretend not to determine. If it be a privilege which all classes of the community may claim with propriety, no consequences can be more natural than those which have hitherto thence arisen, viz: the continual appearance of new sects or denominations.

Burland concluded that liberty was 'carried too far when it enters the sanctuary'.

Behaviour at worship, by both clergy and congregation, was notably less restrained than in Britain. Theatricality reached its peak at the camp prayer meetings, whose description was almost a required item in British accounts of North America. Fanny Trollope attended a meeting at a remote spot in the woods of Indiana, arriving just before midnight. There she found a circle of tents around an open space, surrounded by waiting horses and carriages, with lights hung in the trees:

> Four high frames, constructed in the form of altars, were placed at the four corners of the enclosure; on these were supported layers of earth and sod, on which burned immense fires of blazing pinewood. On one side a rude platform was erected to accommodate the preachers, fifteen of whom attended this meeting, and with very short intervals for necessary refreshment and private devotion, preached in rotation, day and night, from Tuesday to Saturday.

The congregation was praying inside the tents when Mrs Trollope arrived, but at midnight a horn sounded and the clearing was filled with two thousand worshippers, from whom volunteers were exhorted to come to the front of the crowd for the special attention of the ministers:

> How am I to describe the sounds that proceeded from this strange mass of human beings? I know no words which can convey an idea of it. Hysterical sobbings, convulsive groans, shrieks and screams the most appalling, burst forth on all sides. I felt sick with horror . . . Many of these wretched creatures were beautiful young females. The preachers moved among them, at once exciting and soothing their agonies. I heard the muttered 'Sister! dear sister!' I saw the insidious lips approach the cheeks of the unhappy girls; I heard the murmured confessions of the poor victims, and I watched their tormentors, breathing into their ears consolations that tinged the pale cheek with red.

Mrs Trollope soon retired to spend the rest of the night, sleepless, in her carriage, concluding that in England such behaviour by the ministers would demand instant punishment, in the form of 'the salutary discipline of the treadmill'.

Captain Marryat also attended a camp meeting, and was at first a little disappointed to hear a sermon of 'good, sound doctrine'; but later, in one of the tents, he was able to witness the famous scenes of hysteria, with young worshippers convulsed on the ground. He quickly 'hastened away into the forest, for the sight was too painful, too melancholy'.

Whether in relation to children, death, God, the law, or other areas of life, these social and religious practices gave North American society unifying strengths and identities. Their effect countered the divisions of culture, ethnic origin, and distance which ran through the peoples of the United States and Canada. 'They are a mass of people cemented together to a certain degree,' wrote Captain Marryat. The tension between difference and uniformity characterized and enriched society: both were present in a land where strong national identities were maintained over thousands of uncharted miles, while at the same time, in a single street or village, there were proudly different ethnic groups, religions and races.

The continent defied a visiting writer to present a consistent account. Every attempt to generalize observations into aphoristic certainties would be contradicted by a more real and complex pattern of differences: Canada was different from the States, Easterners from Westerners, emigrants from long-settled families.

How could these distinctions be drawn? A lazy solution was simply to relay local prejudice. Captain Marryat provided the following guide to how people referred to their fellow Americans from other states:

Illinois people are termed	Suckers
Missouri	Pukes
Michigan	Wolverines
Indiana	Hoosiers
Kentucky	Corn Crackers
Ohio	Buckeyes etc.

With the broader divisions between territories and groups, many British writers offered their own descriptions. The results combined home truths with blatant prejudice – though it is difficult to know which was which.

New England was the home of the Yankee, the clever, ambitious, unscrupulous American who made the country rich, and envied. Such was the stereotype, confirmed, with some reservations, by Thomas Hamilton, and denied, with some truths admitted, by Tyrone Power:

The New Englanders are not an amiable people. One meets in them much to approve, little to admire, and nothing to love. They may be disliked, however, but they cannot be despised. There is a degree of energy and sturdy independence about them, incompatible with contempt. Abuse them as we may, it must still be admitted they are a singular and original people. Nature, in framing a Yankee, seems to have given him double brains, and half heart.

THOMAS HAMILTON

I do not agree with those who describe the Yankee as a naturally cold-blooded, selfish being. From both the creed and the sumptuary regulations of the rigid moral censors from whom they sprung, they have inherited the practice of a close self-observance and a strict attention to conventional form, which gives a frigid restraint to their air that nevertheless does not sink far beneath the surface . . . In their domestic relations they are proverbial as the kindest husbands and most indulgent fathers; whilst as friends they are found to be, if reasonably wary, at least steadfast, and to be relied on to the uttermost of their professions.

TYRONE POWER

According to Anthony Trollope, travelling Britons would find themselves most welcome and most at ease in the east:

As a general rule of my sojourn in the country, I must declare that I was always happy and comfortable in the eastern cities, and generally unhappy and uncomfortable in the West. I had previously been inclined to think that I should like the roughness of the West, and that in the East I should encounter an arrogance which would have kept me always on the verge of hot water; but in both these surmises I found myself to have been wrong. And I think that most English travellers would come to the same conclusion . . . In all the eastern cities, – I speak of the Eastern cities north of Washington, – a society may be found which must be esteemed as agreeable by Englishmen who like clever genial men, and who love clever pretty women.

Trollope described his unhappiness in the west, where the conventions of the intellectual, courteous society of the east coast were ignored.

In the West I found the men gloomy and silent, – I may almost say sullen. A dozen of them will sit for hours round a stove, speechless. They chew tobacco and ruminate. They are not offended if you speak to them, but they are not pleased. They answer with monosyllables, or, if it be practicable, with a gesture of the head. They care nothing for the graces, – or shall I say, the decencies of life? They are essentially a dirty people. Dirt, untidiness and noise, seem in nowise to afflict them. Things are constantly done before your eyes, which

'The truth of the proverbial saying "there is no God west of the Missouri," is everywhere manifest. The "almighty dollar" is the true divinity, and its worship is universal.'

ISABELLA BIRD

should and might be done behind your back . . . I have eaten in Bedouin tents, and have been ministered to by Turks and Arabs. I have sojourned in the hotels of old Spain, and of Spanish America. I have lived in Connaught, and have taken out my degree in outward abominations. But my education had not reached a point which would enable me to live at my ease in the western states. A man or woman who can do that may be said to have graduated in the highest honours, and to have become absolutely invulnerable, either through the sense of touch, or by the eye, or by the nose. Indifference to appearances is there a matter of pride. A foul shirt is a flag of triumph. A craving for soap and water is as the wail of the weak and the confession of cowardice.

But for all this, Trollope developed a reluctant respect for the western men, recognizing some of the qualities which became standard ingredients of American mythology:

I cannot part with the West without saying in its favour that there is a certain manliness about its men, which gives them a dignity of their own. It is shown in that very indifference of which I have spoken . . . No race of men requires less outward assistance than these pioneers of civilisation. They rarely amuse themselves. Food, newspapers, and brandy-smashes suffice for life; and while these last, whatever may occur, the man is still there in his manhood.

Tyrone Power was an Irish actor whose three year tour of America began in 1833. He too recognized the special qualities of the westerner, living on the edge of white society, and constantly moving to new, unsettled areas:

I like these Western men; their off-hand manner makes you at once at your ease with them: they abound in anecdote growing out of the state in which they live, full of wild frolic and hardy adventure, and they recount these adventures with an exaggeration of figure quite Oriental, in a phraseology peculiar to themselves, and with a manner most humorous.
　　Much among strangers, they have a quick appreciation of character; and, where they take a dislike, are, I have no doubt, mighty troublesome customers; they are, however, naturally courteous, and capable of genuine and inbred kindness.

Isabella Bird, travelling through the Rockies, was full of praise for the courtesy and hospitality she received, but harsh in her account of morality in the west:

People say that on coming from the Eastern States they hardly realise at first the security in which they live. There is no danger and no fear. But the truth of the proverbial saying, 'There is no God west of the Missouri,' is everywhere manifest. The 'almighty dollar' is the true divinity, and its worship is universal. 'Smartness' is the quality thought most of. The boy who 'gets on' by cheating at his lessons is praised for being a 'smart boy,' and his satisfied parents foretell that he will make a 'smart man.' A man who overreaches his neighbour, but who does it so cleverly that the law cannot take hold of him, wins an envied reputation as a 'smart man,' and stories of this species of smartness are told admiringly round every stove.

And Oscar Wilde was unimpressed with western aesthetics:

So infinitesimal did I find the knowledge of Art, west of the Rocky Mountains, that an art patron – one who in his day had been a miner – actually sued the railway company for damages because the plaster cast of Venus de Milo, which he had imported from Paris, had been delivered minus the arms. And, what is more surprising still, he gained his case and the damages.

'In the West, the picturesque is 'the rarest of things ... and the people have even less of the artist feeling than we have.'

MATTHEW ARNOLD

Wilde felt happiest in the American south; from there, writing to American friends in the north, he explained how the southern states offered a welcome break from Yankee efficiency and enterprise:

> I write to you from the beautiful, passionate, ruined South, the land of magnolias and music, of roses and romance: picturesque too in her failure to keep pace with your keen northern pushing intellect; living chiefly on credit, and on the memory of some crushing defeats.

Alexander Mackay, also touring in the south, would have welcomed a little northern energy to maintain southern standards:

> Everything seems filthy in the car, the steamer, and the tavern, as compared with the accommodation met with in the Northern States . . . Even the travellers themselves, taking

them generally, are in their *tout ensemble* less attractive in their appearance, and certainly less refined in their habits, and less particular in their manner, than their Northern fellow-countrymen; whilst not a small proportion of those met with in the extreme South are suspicious in their demeanour, repulsive in their looks, and equivocal in their characters.

Captain Marryat attributed changes in regional character to differences in climate, southerners being especially prone to reckless drinking and fighting because of the extreme heat:

There is a fiery disposition in the southerners which is very remarkable; they are much more easily excited than even the Spaniard or Italian, and their feelings are more violent and unrestrainable . . . It is impossible to imagine a greater difference in character than exists between the hot-blooded southerner and the cold calculating Yankee of the eastern states.

Finally, of course, white southern attitudes were affected by the presence of slavery, as Barbara Bodichon reported:

Miss Juliet was a specimen of a Southern lady. She could not travel alone; she was pale and looked dissipated . . . Miss Juliet could not walk a mile, says few South state American women can; so say all the ladies here in the boat. Slavery makes all labour dishonourable and walking gets to be thought a labour, an exertion.

There was another great social and geographical division to be experienced on any North American trip, that between Canada and the United States. It allowed British visitors to make an almost direct comparison between their own culture and that of the States. Canadian towns like Toronto and Kingston demonstrated the British way on one side of Lake Ontario, while Buffalo and Rochester on the other showed the American.

James Dixon was a Methodist minister who visited North America in 1848 to attend conferences in both the States and Canada. His assessment of the differences between the two national characters reflected badly on Canada, but perhaps worse on Britain, Canada's colonial ruler:

On the American side, the people are all life, elasticity, buoyancy, activity; on the Canadian side we have a people who appear subdued, tame, spiritless, as if living much more under the influence of fear than hope. Again: on the American territory we behold men moving as if they had the idea that their calling was to act, to choose, to govern – at any rate to govern themselves; on the Canada soil we see a race, perhaps more polite than the other, but who seem to live under the impression that their vocation is to receive orders, and obey. Then, on the American side, you are placed in the midst of incessant bustle, agitation; the hotels are filled, coaches are in constant movement, railroad trains passing and repassing with their passengers, while men of business are seen pushing their concerns with impassioned ardour. On the Canada shore we have comparatively still life; delicate, genteel, formal. Moreover, on the American territory, all along the shores of the lakes, the country is being cleared, houses and villages built, works put up, incipient ports opened, and trade begun. On the Canada shore, unbroken forest appears for miles, while the small openings which have been made present themselves to view in a very infantine and feeble state of progress.

There is another striking difference between the Americans and the Canadians. In the first-mentioned country, ideas, sentiments, opinions – in fine, knowledge seems to be considered a common stock. The people sit with their legs across a chair-back, or place them in some other elevated position, and talk at their ease. On the other hand the Canadian people seem to say, 'Do you not know that I am a gentleman? Keep your distance, sir.' . . . They who desire to see nature in its genuine tendencies, will prefer the one; they who admire it most under the restraints of distinctions and fashion, the other.

Barbara Bodichon, in a hotel in Toronto in 1858, had the same complaints about Canadians being disappointingly British:

We are in a hotel full of M.P.'s, officers, divines and all the regular English respectabilities. They are terribly stupid after the Americans who have always something amusing and new to say, whether about the Mormons or California, or slavery, or their preachers or Shakers, etc. Here they talk about 'appointments,' 'places,' 'eldest sons,' 'Governor,' 'Bills' etc.

Captain Marryat described some of these differences, but was able to muster a little enthusiasm for the English virtues of prudence and modesty, and found an economic explanation for Canada's slower development:

The houses and stores at Toronto are not to be compared with those of the American towns opposite. But the Englishman has built according to his means – the American, according to his expectations. The hotels and inns at Toronto are very bad; at Buffalo they are splendid – for the Englishman travels little; the American is ever on the move. The private houses of Toronto are built, according to the English taste and desire of exclusiveness, away from the road, and are embowered in trees; the American, let his house be ever so large, or his plot of ground however extensive, builds within a few feet of the road, that he may see and know what is going on. You do not perceive the bustle, the energy, and activity at

Toronto that you do at Buffalo, nor the profusion of articles in the stores; but it should be remembered that the Americans procure their articles upon credit, whilst at Toronto they proceed more cautiously.

In the far west of the continent, Rudyard Kipling visited Vancouver in 1889, after experiencing American ways in San Francisco. He made the comparison in Canada's favour:

A great sleepiness lies on Vancouver as compared with an American town: men don't fly up and down the streets telling lies, and the spittoons in the delightfully comfortable hotel are unused . . . An American bade me notice the absence of bustle, and was alarmed when in a loud and audible voice I thanked God for it.

CHAPTER SIX

A View from the Settlements

*I have had many conversations with English emigrants in the United
States, and I have never yet found one at all respectable who did not confess
to me that he repented of emigration.*

CAPTAIN MARRYAT

*If you are possessed of rank and money, stay in England . . . If you have
neither rank nor money, get away from it as fast as possible.*

SARAH MYTTON MAURY

The most eager readers of reports from North America were those who were thinking of emigrating. The decision to pack up a life in Europe and cross the sea to make a new one was brave and sometimes irrational. Reliable information was scarce, so letters from new settlers and guidebooks written by travellers and emigrants were studied closely: they included valuable glimpses of everyday life – the price of food, shopping, the climate, the neighbours – and offered a basis on which to decide whether the risk was worth taking.

Among those who decided to emigrate, the most unfortunate were unable even to afford their passage. Their first wages in North America were paid to the captain of their ship, until he had been reimbursed. Until they had a job, they were kept captive on board. Henry Bradshaw Fearon went to visit such a ship full of Dutch emigrants, waiting at a wharf in Philadelphia in 1817. His companion was a boot-maker, looking for someone to hire:

As we ascended the side of this hulk, a most revolting scene of want and misery presented itself . . . Mr. — enquired if there were any shoe-makers on board. The captain advanced: his appearance bespoke his office; he is an American, tall, determined, and with an eye that flashed with Algerine cruelty. He called in the Dutch language for shoe-makers, and never can I forget the scene which followed. The poor fellows came running up with unspeakable delight, no doubt anticipating a relief from their loathsome dungeon. Their clothes, if rags deserve that denomination, actually perfumed the air. Some were without shirts, others had this article of dress, but of a quality as coarse as the worst packing cloth . . . Such is the mercenary barbarity of the Americans who are engaged in this trade, that they crammed into one of those vessels 500 passengers, 80 of whom died on the passage. The price for women is about 70 dollars, men 80 dollars, boys 60 dollars. When they saw at our departure that we had not purchased, their countenances fell to that standard of stupid gloom which seemed to place them a link below rational beings.

Even those who were freely delivered to the site of a new home, were only at the start of their struggles. Charles Dickens, from the comfort of a steamboat on its way to Cincinnati, witnessed the stunned reaction of one family as they were deposited on the river bank to begin a new life:

We stop to set some emigrants ashore. Five men, as many women, and a little girl. All their worldly goods are a bag, a large chest and an old chair: one, old, high-backed, rush-bottomed chair: a solitary settler in itself. They are rowed ashore in the boat, while the vessel stands a little off awaiting its return, the water being shallow. They are landed at the foot of a high bank, on the summit of which are a few log cabins, attainable only by a long winding path. It is growing dusk; but the sun is very red, and shines in the water and on some of the tree-tops like fire.

The men get out of the boat first; help out the women; take out the bag, the chest, the chair; bid the rowers 'goodbye'; and shove the boat off for them. At the first plash of the oars in the water, the oldest woman of the party sits down in the old chair, close to the water's edge, without speaking a word. None of the others sit down, though the chest is large enough for many seats. They all stand where they landed, as if stricken into stone; and look after the boat. So they remain, quite still and silent: the old women and her old chair, in the centre; the bag and chest upon the shore, without anybody heeding them: all eyes fixed upon the boat. It comes alongside, is made fast, the men jump on board, the engine is put in motion, and we go hoarsely on again. There they stand yet, without the motion of a hand. I can see them, through my glass, when, in the distance and increasing darkness, they are mere specks to the eye: lingering there still: the old woman in the old chair, and the rest about her: not stirring in the least degree. And thus I slowly lose them.

Imagination gave the new land attractions it could never offer in reality, and arriving emigrants were often disappointed, if not plainly shocked at what they found. Anne Langton, an educated Englishwoman who travelled to Canada to join her recently emigrated brother, John, in 1837, had been well-informed by his letters about his circumstances. But still the first sight of the primitive settlement came as something of a blow:

What most strikes me is a greater degree of roughness in the farming, buildings, gardens, fences, and especially roads, than I had expected. But when one looks at the wild woods around, and thinks that from such a wilderness the present state of things has been brought out by a few hands, and how much there is for those few hands to be constantly doing, one's surprise vanishes, and one rather wonders that so much has been done, than that so much remains to be done. This certainly is a country where the virtue of patience will not languish for want of exercise.

New settlers like Anne Langton were suddenly living in much closer touch with nature than they were used to; the buffer of civilization had been removed. They found themselves owning a few acres of land, sometimes only partly 'cleared' of trees and surrounded by a view of uncut, featureless forest in all directions. They had to build their home, grow their food,

'Persons of idle and indolent habits, of no regular trade or business, of weak or delicate constitutions, of wavering or unstable minds . . . ought never to enter Canada.'

REVD ISAAC FIDLER

cook, stay healthy, and endure a longer and more severe winter than they had ever known. It was a fight for survival, and it is surprising there was ever time to write, either for the record, or to reassure relatives back home. But diaries and letters poured from the furthest settlements, often written by the sons and daughters of middle-class English families. They were the lifeline that kept their writers in touch with the cultured, leisured people they once were, and who, if the farm prospered, they might one day become again.

Catherine Parr Traill, herself an English emigrant, wrote her *Canadian Settler's Guide* in 1855 to warn those planning a life in the backwoods of the difficulties they might face. In particular, she pointed out possible marital strains that their new life could place on a couple:

> Whatever be the determination of the intended emigrant, let him not exclude from his entire confidence the wife of his bosom . . . She ought not to be dragged as an unwilling sacrifice at the shrine of duty from home, kindred and friends, without her full consent: the difficulties as well as the apparent advantages ought to be laid candidly before her, and her advice and opinion asked.

Such advice was apparently needed: Anna Brownell Jameson reported from Canada that 'I never met with *one* woman recently settled here, who considered herself happy in her new home and country.' Jameson arrived in Toronto in 1836 as the wife of the newly-appointed Attorney-General of Ontario, but her marriage was not a happy one. She left her husband to explore the wilder northern parts of the province. On her travels, she met a man who had lived in the bush for five years; perhaps echoing her own experience in leaving Europe for a less sophisticated life in Canada, she quoted his warning that for the wife of a settler, the imagined life contrasted painfully with the reality:

> A cottage in the wild woods – solitude and love – the world forgetting, by the world forgot – the deer come skipping by - the red Indian brings game, and lays it at her feet – how pretty and how romantic! And for the first few months, perhaps the first year, all goes well; but how goes it the next, and the next? I have observed with regard to the women who come out, that they do well enough the first year, and some even the second; but the third is generally fatal: and the worst with you women – or the best shall I not say? – is that you cannot, and do not, forget domestic ties left behind. We men go out upon our land, or to the chase, and the women, poor souls, sit, and sew, and *think*. You have seen Mrs. A. and Mrs. B. who came out here, as I well remember, full of health and bloom – what are they now? premature old women, sickly, care-worn, without nerve or cheerfulness.

Perseverance and the passage of time could turn these complaints into mere grumbles. Henry Bradshaw Fearon concluded that after a month in the States, an Englishman would often deeply regret having left home, but that his life would soon improve, and his feelings change:

> Could I see him in twelve months from the present time, I think his condition would be, if I may judge from others, something like the following: – saved fourteen guineas; living in two small rooms; independent of his master, and his master of him; thinks the Americans a very dirty and disagreeable people, and hates them from his soul; would be delighted to see old England again, and smoke his pipe and drink his pint, and talk politics with the cobbler, and abuse the taxes; and then he remembers that he is in America, where he cannot endure the thoughts of having his bones buried; thinks of returning to England, where his wife is anxious to go, in order that she may drink tea and gossip with her old neighbours; then they both conjure up their former sea sickness, their fear of being drowned, the money that their passage would cost, and that when they got to Hull, his most laborious application would not more than provide them with a bare existence. He then determines to remain in America, keep the money which he has saved, add as much more to it as he can, and make himself as contented and happy as lies in his power.

Homesickness and the traumas of setting up a new life could be overcome if character and family unity were set against the uncertainties. Captain Marryat visited a model settler's home in Canada:

> We called upon a man who had been in the bush but a year or so; he had a wife and six children. He was young and healthy, and although he had been used to a life of *literary* idleness, he had made up his mind to the change, and taken up the axe – a thing very few people can do. I never saw a person more cheerful and contented. He had already cleared away about fifteen acres, and had procured a summer crop from off a portion of it the year before, having no other assistance than his two boys, one thirteen and the other fourteen years old, healthy, but not powerfully built lads . . . I went with the man into his log-hut, which was large and convenient, and found his wife working at her needle, and three little girls all as busy as bees; the eldest of these girls was not twelve years old, yet she cooked, baked, washed, and, with the assistance of her two little sisters, did all that was required for the household . . .
> We promised to call upon him on our return, which we did. We found him sitting with his wife in his log-house; it was five o'clock in the afternoon; he told us 'work was over now, and that the children had gone into the bush to play.' They had all worked from five o'clock in the morning, and had since learnt their lessons. We heard their laughter ringing in the woods at a distance.

'We visited one farm, which interested us particularly from its wild and lonely situation . . . These people were indeed independent, Robinson Crusoe was hardly more so, and they eat and drink abundantly; but yet it seemed to me that there was something awful and almost unnatural in their loneliness.'

FANNY TROLLOPE

Marryat remarked that if this man had been a bachelor, he would probably have become an alcoholic. But middle-class English bachelors also prospered in the backwoods if they could structure their lives with sufficient discipline. John Langton was an industrious English emigrant who set up home for himself in the backwoods of Ontario, where he lived for four years before his sister and parents joined him. He described the solitary life of the early days, with its almost obsessive rituals:

I rise at an hour varying from five to seven. Having dressed I clean the house whilst the kettle is boiling and after breakfast I smoke a cigar and read as long as it lasts; I then wash up the accumulated plates, etc., of the twenty-four hours and set to work at chopping firewood, joinering or whatever may be in hand at the time. At an hour before sunset, which I have come to calculate very accurately, I begin cooking, bringing in a pile of firewood, sweeping out the house, etc., in the intervals; and I rarely fail to have finished my dinner just as it gets dark. Another cigar's time is then devoted to meditation and digestion, and after reading, writing or sewing for half a candle, I go to bed.

The Oxford-educated bachelor Thomas Need, a neighbour of Langton's, also recorded his daily routine at a time when his farm was under construction:

I rose early and worked in the garden until breakfast, then read for a couple of hours; afterwards chopped firewood in the shade, until three o'clock when I dined, and resumed my studies for an hour: the next two hours were passed with the woodmen, in overlooking their work, and at six o'clock I took tea, and afterwards floated about the lake in my canoe, with or without a gun, until nine or ten o'clock, when I retired to bed and slept most soundly: my health was very good, my spirits even, and I was well satisfied with my condition.

Bringing capital from England, Need was able to employ men to help him set up his farm; he also brought a servant, who presumably supervised his 'dining'. However primitive the settler's life, one requirement to make a success of it seems to have been a sense of values outside the limited world of the cleared forest. In an exhaustive list of what is needed to furnish a simple log house, Catherine Parr Traill's *Settler's Guide* concludes, with some force:

A few prints, or pictures, in frames of oak or black walnut, should not be omitted, if you can bring such ornaments with you. These things are sources of pleasure to yourselves, and of interest to others. They are intellectual luxuries, that even the very poorest man regards with delight, and possesses if he can, to adorn his cottage walls, however lowly that cottage may be.

Educated British settlers brought their own culture. There was even a 'Universities Club' in the backwoods of Ontario, admitting only men from Oxford or Cambridge. It didn't last long, but even the suggestion that such an idea might be serious was an indication of the settlers' determination to bring civilization, as they saw it, with them. Thomas Need was grateful for his collection of old university books:

Several of the classics, which on their shelves at Oxford were rather looked at than into, were now treated with the attention they deserve; and in the solitude of the Bush, it was no

The Writers

SUSANNA MOODIE (1803–85) was the youngest of six daughters of a wealthy Suffolk merchant. She was already a published writer when she emigrated to Canada in 1834 with her husband, Dunbar Moodie. After years of struggle and set-backs in the backwoods, the Moodies moved to a small town, where she enjoyed a more tranquil existence. An English childhood friend, J. Ewing Ritchie, published an account of his own trip to Canada in 1884, including a visit to the Moodies' home: 'The sprightly lady of 1834, eager and enthusiastic, had become an elderly one in 1884; yet time had dealt gently with her, and her youth seemed to revive as she talked of her old Suffolk home . . . But she has no wish to come back to England – her family are all well settled in Canada. She told me anecdotes of myself when a boy that I had quite forgotten.' Moodie died later that year, but her experiences as a settler, recorded in *Roughing it in the Bush* (1852), live on as a classic of Canadian literature.

THE WRITERS

CATHERINE PARR TRAILL (1802–99) was a sister of Susanna Moodie. She too married an officer and emigrated to Canada, a week after the Moodies. Her books, *The Backwoods of Canada* (1836) and *The Canadian Settler's Guide* (1855) are more optimistic than Moodie's, being full of practical advice to future emigrants, on everything from making soap, to saving the life of a child with dysentery. She suffered the difficulties of her family's early days in Canada with a strong sense of destiny, of building for a future which, if she could see Ontario today, she might feel had indeed materialized: 'some century hence how different will this spot appear! I can picture it to my imagination with fertile fields and groves of trees planted by hand of taste. All will be different; our present rude dwellings will have given place to others of a more elegant style of architecture, and comfort and grace will rule the scene which is now a forest wild.' Traill became an expert on Canadian flora. Her books on wild flowers brought her fame, and recognition in the form of gifts from both the British and Canadian governments, who gave her, respectively, £100, and an island on her beloved Otonabee River.

light pleasure to re-peruse scenes and passages, every one of which was pregnant with some cherished association of school or college.

For women, there were complicated questions about servants: where should they go in a log cabin which was often only one room? And should their mistress work with them, as would seem natural in the New World, but so unnatural in the Old?

The social hierarchy was almost invisible, which was distressing to those who felt they would naturally find themselves near its pinnacle. Sometimes there was a welcome chance to suggest the existence of such an order: Anne Langton's elderly mother had recently emigrated from a prosperous home outside Liverpool and felt deprived of her usual charitable exercises, as her daughter reported:

I took a walk as far as the Dukes' to enquire after the baby, who had been an invalid, and to carry a small donation of clothing. It had rather weighed on my mother's mind that she had so few opportunities for the exercise of charity, and she was somewhat pleased, I think, to hear that this family was a little complaining at being poorly off in some respects; but she had not had full satisfaction in her bounty, finding that they keep a servant.

Settlers had to help each other, particularly in the jobs which required many hands. The 'raising' of a new settler's first house became an institutionalized party, the 'bee', sometimes known in the States as a 'frolic', to which local people came, and gave a day's work, cutting and lifting logs; their pay was in food and drink, provided by the newcomers. The intention was to complete the log cabin in a day, but alcohol often slowed progress, as William Thomson, an itinerant Scot, witnessed at a new settlement near Toronto:

At first they went to work moderately and with quietness, but after the whisky had been handed about several times they got very uproarious – swearing, shouting, tumbling down, and sometimes like to fight . . . most of them were drunk and all of them excited. The manner in which they use their axes was a 'caution.' Many accidents happen, and lives are frequently lost on these occasions, both from accidents and quarrels . . .

The walls of a house, 15 by 26, and 12 feet high, were up before night; and some of the nearest neighbours were to return next day and cut out the doors and windows . . . I left them, thinking I would not like the foundation of my house laid, with so many oaths to consecrate it as I had heard that day.

Settlers who were able to resist the immediate consolation of whisky were rewarded: year by year, more crops would be harvested, livestock would increase, the settlers would become more skilled in their work, and the neighbourhood would 'fill up', bringing more stores, a school, a church, better roads and a rise in the price of land. Thomas Need described precisely the transformation of forest into town:

> At first, some one or two adventurers, possessed of a little capital, purchase a few acres of land on the bank of a river or stream, where, in the provincial idiom, there is good water power; two or three rude huts or shanties are erected, and a small clearing made in the forest; by degrees, others are attracted to the spot: the original settler, meanwhile, has turned a little money, and embarks it in a saw mill; this induces many to come into the neighbourhood, from the facility it offers for building. Then, as the settlement increases, some bold man is persuaded to erect a grist or flour mill, which again serves as an attraction; a growing population requires the necessaries of life at hand; stores are opened, a tavern licenced, and in a few years a thriving village, or, as in the case of Peterboro', an important town, springs up in the heart of the forest.

The middle-class emigrants were often impatient with progress, fast though it was, and they gravitated towards the established towns, abandoning the manual work which had been their introduction to their new country. After years in the bush, Susanna Moodie returned to quiet urban life when her husband was appointed Sheriff of Hastings County, Ontario, in 1840. The family moved to the small town of Belleville, on the sheltered Bay of Quinte, near Lake Ontario. Their journey into town was a revelation to the Moodies' eldest son, then five years old, who had never before left the backwoods. 'Are the houses come to see one another?' he asked on seeing Belleville for the first time. 'How did they all meet here?' For his mother, the change was a blessing, and a relief from worry and work, but still it brought regrets:

> For seven years I had lived out of the world entirely; my person had been rendered coarse by hard work and exposure to the weather. I looked double the age I really was, and my hair was already thickly sprinkled with grey. I clung to my solitude. I did not like to be dragged from it to mingle in gay scenes, in a busy town, and with gaily-dressed people. I was no longer fit for the world; I had lost all relish for the pursuits and pleasures which are so essential to its votaries; I was contented to live and die in obscurity.

In fact, Susanna Moodie lived for forty-five years after her return to society, and published two autobiographical books, five novels, and some fiction for children. Her experiences as a settler made her name, by conveying vividly the physical and emotional hardships of that life, so different from the beguiling fantasy of a simple existence in harmony with nature. In describing her early days as an emigrant, Moodie recalled, somewhat apologetically, part of a poem she wrote when she was at her lowest ebb in the Canadian backwoods:

Oh! land of waters, how my spirit tires,
    In the dark prison of thy boundless woods;
No rural charm poetic thought inspires,
    No music murmurs in thy mighty floods;
Though vast the features that compose thy frame,
Turn where we will, the landscape's still the same.

The swampy margin of thy inland seas,
    The eternal forest girdling either shore,
Its belt of dark pines sighing in the breeze,
    And rugged field, with rude huts dotted o'er,
Show cultivation unimproved by art,
That sheds a barren chillness on the heart.

CHAPTER SEVEN
AMERICAN LANDSCAPES

On first arriving, I thought the many tree covered hills around, very beautiful, but long before my departure, I felt so weary of the confined view, that Salisbury Plain would have been an agreeable variety.

FANNY TROLLOPE

The uncultivated landscape of North America presented a challenge to a European's romantic view of nature: the untouched forests were undeniably an obstacle to the prosperous and comfortable conduct of human life; and, surprisingly, they were not even thought 'picturesque'. Fanny Trollope complained about the dense barrier of vegetation between the trees: 'it is this circumstance which makes the "eternal forests" of American so detestable.' Nevertheless, she and her party, living in Cincinnati, sometimes forgot their disappointment, and, with sandwiches in a basket, set off up one of the hills surrounding the town for an afternoon's walking and sketching, as if they were taking a stroll on Hampstead Heath:

We were determined to enjoy ourselves, and forward we went, crunching knee deep through aboriginal leaves . . . We decided on reposing awhile on the trunk of a fallen tree; being all considerably exhausted, the idea of sitting down on this tempting log was conceived and executed simultaneously by the whole party, and the whole party sunk together through its treacherous surface into a mass of rotten rubbish that had formed part of the pith and marrow of the eternal forest a hundred years before.

We were by no means the only sufferers by the accident; frogs, lizards, locusts, katiedids, beetles, and hornets, had the whole of their various tenements disturbed, and testified their displeasure very naturally by annoying us as much as possible in return; we were bit, we were stung, we were scratched; and when, at last, we succeeded in raising ourselves from the venerable ruin, we presented as woeful a spectacle as can well be imagined. We shook our (not ambrosial) garments, and panting with heat, stings, and vexation, moved a few paces from the scene of our misfortune, and again sat down; but this time it was upon the solid earth.

    We had no sooner began to 'chew the cud' of the bitter fancy that had beguiled us to these mountain solitudes than a new annoyance assailed us. A cloud of mosquitoes gathered round, and while each sharp proboscis sucked our blood, they teased us with their humming chorus, till we lost all patience, and started again on our feet, pretty firmly resolved never to try the *al fresco* joys of an American forest again.

Anthony Trollope, touring America thirty years later, in 1861, picked up his mother's theme:

We, in England, when we read and speak of the primeval forests of America, are apt to form pictures in our minds of woodland glades, with spreading oaks and green mossy turf beneath, – of scenes than which nothing that God has given us is more charming. But these forests are not after that fashion; they offer no allurement to the lover, no solace to the melancholy man of thought. The ground is deep with mud, or overflown with water. The soil and the river have no defined margins. Each tree, though full of the forms of life, has all the appearance of death. Even to the outward eye they seem to be laden with ague, fever, sudden chills, and pestilential malaria.

This attitude was more than just a quirk of the Trollope family. Even Frances Wright, usually gushing in her praise for all things American, had her reservations on this subject: she reported that when a firm forest floor could be found, a pleasant walk beneath the trees was possible, 'at least those will think so whose eyes are not palled with their eternal contemplation'. This confining, inescapable quality of trees seemed to depress the settlers as much as the visitors:

One wood is the exact picture of another; the uniformity dreary in the extreme. There are no green vistas to be seen; no grassy glades beneath the bosky oaks, on which the deer browse, and the gigantic shadows sleep in the sunbeams. A stern array of rugged trunks, a tangled maze of scrubby underbrush, carpetted winter and summer with a thick layer of withered buff leaves, form the general features of a Canadian forest.

SUSANNA MOODIE

Survival in the backwoods depended on removing the trees, and letting the sunlight warm the earth; Charles Weld explained that 'war to extermination against the forest is the settler's rule'. Catherine Parr Traill concluded: 'man appears to contend with the trees of the forest as though they were his most obnoxious enemies.' Thomas Need, supervising the clearing of trees for his home in the forest, also struggled with his conscience:

'When the woodman with his axe enters these territories for the first time, he cannot resist the impression that he is about to commit a trespass on the virgin lovliness of nature, that he is going to bring into captivity what has been free for centuries.'
REBECCA BURLAND

As I approached the settlement, the heavy fall of the axe gave notice that the work of demolition was going forward; several hemlock and other soft-wooded trees lay stretched along the shore; and I confess it was with a somewhat English feeling of sorrow for their fate that I stepped out amongst them. A glance at the Falls, however, and the clear blue lake beyond, through the opening, reassured me, and I soon entered into the exultant feelings of the choppers, as one after another the noblest among these ancient lords of the soil groaned under the stroke of the axe, trembled for a few seconds, and fell.

This war of attrition, in which human forces laboriously beat back the forest, produced a new landscape around the settlements, to many, almost as depressing as the one it replaced:

There prevailed a most uncomfortable appearance of bleakness or rawness, and a total absence of picturesque beauty in these villages; whose dreary aspect was much heightened by the black sort of gigantic wall formed of the abrupt edge of the forest, choked up with underwood, now for the first time exposed to the light of the sun . . . Even in the cultivated fields, the tops of the stumps were seen poking their black snouts above the young grain, like a shoal of seals.

BASIL HALL

The tree stumps were almost immovable, and were usually left to decay, which could take up to ten years. Charles Dickens, watching their curious shapes in the twilight, from a stage-coach, found them a source of imaginary illusions: 'now, there is a Grecian urn erected in the centre of a lonely field; now there is a woman weeping at a tomb; now a very commonplace old gentleman in a white waistcoat, with a thumb thrusting into each arm-hole of his coat; now a student poring on a book; now a crouching negro; now a horse, a dog, a cannon, an armed man.' In the fields, stumps were safe enough, but there were also plenty left on the roads, where they were a hazard: to Dickens they were a useful stimulant for a dosy driver:

We had the comfort of knowing, at least, that there was no danger of his falling asleep, for every now and then a wheel would strike against an unseen stump with such a jerk, that he was fain to hold on pretty tight and pretty quick, to keep himself upon the box.

To be 'stumped' was to have one's carriage overturned on a new road; the expression, as Captain Marryat explained to his readers, was adapted by Americans for general use, in phrases such as 'well I am stumped this time'.

The battle against the forest was powered by money; sometimes development was so fast that a sizeable town would emerge without any village having existed on the site. Basil Hall watched the birth of the booming town of Rochester, New York, in 1827:

As fast as the trees were cut down, they were stripped of their branches and drawn off by oxen, sawed into planks, or otherwise fashioned to the purposes of building, without one moment's delay. There was little or no exaggeration, therefore, in supposing . . . that the same fir which might be waving about in full life and vigour in the morning, should be cut down, dragged into daylight, squared, framed, and before night, be hoisted up to make a beam or rafter to some tavern, or factory, or store, at the corner of a street, which twenty-four hours before had existed only on paper.

Such was the reality of much of North America's changing landscape, at least in the white settler's struggle with it. Only when most of the trees had been removed could the visitor enjoy its tamed beauty, and imagine a paradise. The newly-arrived Robert Louis Stevenson surveyed the prosperous countryside of Pennsylvania in 1879 from the viewing platform of a train:

'Our humble home, already near completed, stood, surrounded by the eternal forest. A few trees had been cleared in its immediate vicinity, just sufficient to allow the workmen to proceed, and to prevent the fall of any tree injuring the building.'

SUSANNA MOODIE

There was not a cloud; the sunshine was baking; yet in the woody river-valleys among which we wound our way, the atmosphere preserved a sparkling freshness till late in the afternoon. It had an inland sweetness and variety to one newly from the sea; it smelt of woods, rivers, and the delved earth. There, though in so far a country, were airs from home. I stood on the platform by the hour; and as I saw one after another, pleasant villages, carts upon the highway and fishers by the stream, and heard cockcrows and cheery voices in the distance, and beheld the sun, no longer shining blankly on the plains of ocean, but striking among shapely hills and his light dispersed and coloured by a thousand accidents of form and surface, I began to exult with myself upon this rise in life like a man who had come into a rich estate. And when I had asked the name of a river from the brakesman, and heard that it was called Susquehanna, the beauty of the name seemed to be part and parcel of the beauty of the land. As when Adam with divine fitness named the creatures, so this word Susquehanna was at once accepted by the fancy. That was the name, as no other could be, for that shining river and desirable valley.

This, then, was the American Eden, constructed by human efforts, seen from the detachment of a passing train, and cast in the image of home. The early tree-bound settler had seldom found the natural landscape as welcoming.

There were exceptions: those who settled on the prairies of Wisconsin and Iowa were among the most fortunate. Captain Marryat reported that the natural state of the prairies was almost ideal: clearing of timber was unnecessary, cattle fattened fast, and 'the soil is so fertile that you have but to turn it up to make it yield grain to any extent'. The big, empty vistas of the mid-west presented the visitor with subtly differing flat landscapes all the way to the Rockies; the prairies were a blank canvas on which travellers could project their own thoughts and emotions. Marryat's admiration prompted a reverie which took him back to his days of glory at sea:

> Look round in every quarter of the compass, and there you are as if on the ocean – not a landmark, not a vestige of anything human but yourself. Instead of sky and water, it is one vast field, bounded only by the horizon, its surface gently undulating like the waves of the ocean; and as the wind (which always blows fresh on the prairies) bows down the heads of the high grass, it gives you the idea of a running swell.

Almost all writers, naval or otherwise, compared the prairie landscape to the sea, often with an element of dream-like confusion. Those with sea-faring experience, like Basil Hall, were best able to fill out the nautical details:

> The resemblance to the sea, which some of the Prairies exhibited, was really most singular . . . There is one spot in particular, near the middle of the Grand Prairie, if I recollect rightly, where the ground happened to be of the rolling character above alluded to, and where, excepting in the article of colour – and that was not widely different from the tinge of some seas – the similarity was so very striking, that I almost forgot where I was. This deception was heightened by a circumstance which I had often heard mentioned, but the force of which, perhaps, none but a seaman could fully estimate; I mean the appearance of the distant insulated trees, as they gradually rose above the horizon, or receded from our view. They were so exactly like strange sails heaving in sight, that I am sure, if two or three sailors had been present, they would almost have agreed as to what canvas these magical vessels were carrying.

For Robert Louis Stevenson, fresh from a traumatic ocean crossing in steerage, the same comparison led to a vivid, surrealist description of his situation:

We were at sea – there is no other adequate expression – on the plains of Nebraska. I made my observatory on the top of a fruit-waggon, and sat by the hour upon that perch to spy about me, and to spy in vain for something new. It was a world almost without a feature; an empty sky, an empty earth; front and back, the line of railway stretched from horizon to horizon, like a cue across a billiard-board; on either hand, the green plain ran till it touched the skirts of heaven. Along the track innumerable wild sunflowers, no bigger than a crown-piece, bloomed in a continuous flower-bed; grazing beasts were seen upon the prairie at all degrees of distance and diminution; and, now and again we might perceive a few dots besides the railroad which grew more and more distinct as we drew nearer till they turned into wooden cabins, and then dwindled and dwindled in our wake until they melted into their surroundings, and we were once more alone upon the billiard-board. The train toiled

'Nature had so arranged it that man should have all difficulties cleared from before him, and have but little to do but to take possession and enjoy.'
CAPTAIN MARRYAT, ON THE AMERICAN PRAIRIES

over this infinity like a snail; and being the one thing moving, it was wonderful what huge proportions it began to assume in our regard. It seemed miles in length, and either end of it within but a step of the horizon. Even my own body or my own head seemed a great thing in that emptiness. I note the feeling the more readily as it is the contrary of what I have read of in the experience of others. Day and night, above the roar of the train, our ears were kept busy with the incessant chirp of grasshoppers – a noise like the winding up of countless clocks and watches, which began after a while to seem proper to that land.

Dickens found the prairie 'like a sea without water', but refused to recommend it: 'I would say to every man who can't see a prairie – go to Salisbury plain, Marlborough downs, or any of the broad, high, open lands near the sea. Many of them are fully as impressive; and Salisbury plain is *decidedly* more so.' Charles Kingsley, travelling south to St Louis, also found a more domestic comparison: the prairies were 'like the Norfolk fens without the ditches'.

The British liked to think of themselves as lovers of nature, but these homely landscapes were perhaps more appealing than the vast untamed wildernesses of the huge continent. While British tourists discussed the landscape, and looked for the perfect spot from which to sketch it, the Americans made less of a show of appreciating nature. Basil Hall, visiting Trenton Falls, New York, with a party of Americans, complained that they found nothing to talk about after their walk to the beauty spot, an excursion which, 'in any other country would, I am sure, have furnished conversation for hours afterwards'.

Charles Mackay was outraged by overhearing an American tourist in a hotel at Niagara who was more impressed with the suspension bridge over the river than with the Falls themselves:

'Niagara is a handsome thing,' said a guest at the Monteagle House to his neighbour; 'but what is it to the bridge? The bridge! why, I hold *that* to be the finest thing in all God's universe!' It was no engineer who spake thus, but a man from a dry-goods store in Chicago, and doubtless a very worthy man too: though, if I could have had my will of him . . . I would have inflicted summary justice upon him, and in the very scene and moment of his offence deprived him for ever of all the rights of citizenship.

And Rudyard Kipling, on an excursion to Yellowstone National Park, Wyoming, was impressed by the grandeur of the scenery, but infuriated by the luke-warm response of his American fellow-tourists: 'some of the persons in the coach remarked that the scenery was "elegant". Wherefore, even at the risk of my own life, I did urgently desire an accident and the massacre of some of the more prominent citizens.' Yet this was the same traveller who, a few days earlier, had decided not to explore further north than British Columbia because he had discovered he was 'surfeited with scenery'. Kipling was only in Yellowstone because he had been warned about the beauty of Alaska:

> There is a great deal in the remark of a discontented traveller: 'When you have seen a pine forest, a bluff, a river, and a lake you have seen all the scenery of western America. Sometimes the pine is three hundred feet high, and sometimes the rock is, and sometimes the lake is a hundred miles long. But it's all the same, don't you know. I'm getting sick of it.' I dare not say getting sick. I'm only tired . . . Men said if I went to Alaska I should see islands even more wooded, snow-peaks loftier, and rivers more lovely than those around me. That decided me not to go to Alaska.

CHAPTER EIGHT
INDIANS

On returning home, I found a party of Indians encamped on my property near the lake. At first, I felt very much disposed to assert my manorial rights, and dislodge them; but on cooler reflection, it struck me that, in their eyes, I might seem the intruder, and that on the whole it would be politic as well as charitable to leave them in peace, and live on kindly terms with them during their sojourn.

THOMAS NEED

According to Oscar Wilde, 'English people are far more interested in American barbarism than they are in American civilisation.' Certainly, this century, barbarism has dominated European perceptions of relations between the white population of North America and the native Indian peoples. Popular westerns and a continuing realization of the long-term effects of white settlement on the lives of the native peoples reinforce a picture of bloody conflict and devastation.

In the last century, many British writers were already noticing the havoc wreaked on the Indians by white society; sometimes they used their observations as another chance for a self-righteous jab at the Americans. But there were other notes in the chorus of reports about Indians, who formed a colourful chapter in the more ambitious books of American memoirs. There were personal encounters with Indian people, in which writers often described with the greatest respect, the manners and customs of the tribes. There were tales of cooperation between white people and native people, as they learned to live next to each other. And there were genuine friendships. These local experiences of successful co-existence were undermined by social forces outside the control of individuals from either group.

Charles Dickens, on an Ohio steamboat, noticed that as well as 'the usual dreary crowd of passengers', there was an Indian chief, with whom, he reported, 'I had the pleasure of a long conversation'. Dickens was amused when the chief sent over his card by way of introduction:

He spoke English perfectly well, though he had not begun to learn the language, he told me, until he was a young man grown. He had read many books; and Scott's poetry

'The Indians are as proud of their descent (and with good reason) as we, in Europe, are of ours.'
CAPTAIN MARRYAT

appeared to have left a strong impression on his mind: especially the opening of *The Lady of the Lake,* and the great battle scene in *Marmion,* in which, no doubt from the congeniality of the subjects to his own pursuits and tastes, he had great interest and delight . . . He was dressed in our ordinary everyday costume, which hung about his fine figure loosely, and with indifferent grace. On my telling him that I regretted not to see him in his own attire, he threw up his right arm, for a moment, as though he were brandishing some heavy weapon, and answered, as he let it fall again, that his race were losing many things beside their dress, and would soon be seen upon the earth no more.

Another meeting, reported by Anna Brownell Jameson shortly after her arrival in Toronto in 1836, showed Indian people remarkably capable of adapting themselves to the expectations of the settlers. Jameson had requested the local Indian agent, Colonel Givens, to arrange a visit, and the Colonel obliged, producing a chief and two others for inspection at Jameson's home:

The chief wore a blanket coat, and leggings, and a blanket hood with a peak from which depended a long black eagle plume; stout moccasins or shoes of undressed deer-skin completed his attire . . . Chairs being presented, they sat down at once (though, as Colonel Givens said, they would certainly have preferred the floor), and answered with a grave and quiet dignity the compliments and questions addressed to them. Their deportment was taciturn and self-possessed, and their countenances melancholy; that of the chief was by far the most intelligent. They informed me that they were Chippewas from the neighbourhood of Lake Huron; that the hunting season had been unsuccessful; that their tribe was suffering the extremity of hunger and cold; and that they had come to beg from their Great Father the Governor rations of food, and a supply of blankets for their women and children. They had walked over the snow, in their snow-shoes, from the lake, one hundred and eighty miles, and for the last forty-eight hours none of them had tasted food. A breakfast of cold meat, bread, and beer, was immediately ordered for them; and though they had certainly never beheld in their lives the arrangement of an European table, and were besides half-famished, they sat down with unembarrassed tranquillity, and helped themselves to what they wished, with the utmost propriety.

Each, on parting, held out his hand to me, and the chief, with grave earnestness, prayed for the blessing of the Great Spirit on me and my house. On the whole, the impression they left, though amusing and exciting from its mere novelty, was melancholy. The sort of desperate resignation in their swarthy countenances, their squalid, dingy habiliments, and their forlorn story, filled me with pity, and, I may add, disappointment; and all my previous impressions of the independent children of the forest are for the present disturbed.

The most genuine friendships between white people and Indians occurred when the white people were near neighbours of the Indians, and also living off the land. Catherine Parr Traill met members of the Chippewa tribe who lived near her newly-built log house in Ontario. Along with members of her family, she was invited by a hunter chief into a large Indian wigwam on a winter's night. The Indians had evidently been taught Christianity:

> We had so often listened with pleasure to the Indians singing their hymns of a Sunday night that I requested some of them to sing to us; the old hunter nodded assent; and, without removing his pipe, with the gravity and phlegm of a Dutchman, issued his commands, which were as instantly obeyed by the younger part of the community, and a chorus of rich voices filled the little hut with a melody that thrilled to our very hearts.
>
> The hymn was sung in the Indian tongue, a language that is peculiarly sweet and soft in its cadences, and seems to be composed with many vowels . . . I wish you could have witnessed the scene; I think you would not easily have forgotten it. I was pleased with the air of deep reverence that sat on the faces of the elders of the Indian family as they listened to the voices of their children singing praise and glory to the God and Saviour they had learned to fear and love.

'I observe, while loitering among them, that they seldom raise their voices, and they pronounce several words much more softly than we write them. Wigwam, a house, they pronounce wee-ga-waum – lengthening the vowels, and softening the aspirates.'
ANNA BROWNELL JAMESON

Traill's sister and Canadian neighbour, Susanna Moodie, also recorded her experiences of the local Indians: 'we met them with confidence; our dealings with them were conducted with the strictest integrity; and they became attached to our persons, and in no single instance ever destroyed the good opinion we entertained of them.' The Moodies knew the Indians well enough to learn their nick-names for the other white settlers. Indians would visit the Moodie home almost every week, and were invited to dinner, over which there would be intense discussions about the fixtures and fittings of the house. The Indians wanted to learn about every object they saw, what it was used for and what it was made of. One instance gives an example of the harmless, perhaps helpful, transfer of white culture to the Indians:

> With a large map of Canada, they were infinitely delighted. In a moment they recognised every bay and headland in Ontario, and almost screamed with delight when, following the course of the Trent with their fingers, they came to their own lake.
>
> How eagerly each pointed out the spot to his fellows; how intently their black heads were bent down, and their dark eyes fixed upon the map! What strange, uncouth exclamations of surprise burst from their lips as they rapidly repeated the Indian names for every lake and river on this wonderful piece of paper.

Moodie reported that 'the Indian never forgets a kindness'; her family enjoyed the generosity of their Indian friends when their own fortunes were at a low ebb after crop failures and illness. The Indians gave them food while their white neighbours, she said, 'looked coldly upon us'. And she was touched by the Indians' discretion: they would pretend the gifts were for the Moodie's children, or simply drop them at the door unseen, 'thinking that receiving a present from a poor Indian might hurt our feelings'. For all this, Mrs Moodie was aware of the long-term effects of her society on the Indian way of life:

> Often have I grieved that people with such generous impulses should be degraded and corrupted by civilised men; that a mysterious destiny involves and hangs over them, pressing them back into the wilderness, and slowly and surely sweeping them from the earth.

Indians met on or near their own territory were often reported as impressive, generous and wise. But found washed up on the edge of a new culture in which they played no part, they presented quite a different picture. Isabella Bird, seeing a crowd of ragged Indians, 'hideous and filthy and swarming with vermin', on a train crossing the Rockies, described them as 'a most impressive incongruity in the midst of the tokens of an omnipotent civilisation'. Lady Theodora Guest, waiting on the platform at Salt Lake City station, gathered a similarly fleeting impression:

'They are strong and active; patient of fatigue and privation, and always willing to accompany the white-man to the chase; but neither entreaties, bribes, nor threats, will induce them, under the circumstances, to help him in his farm or garden.'

THOMAS NEED

We interviewed some horrible-looking, dirty, miserable Indians, of the Ute tribe, who were hanging about the station. They were a degraded-looking, hopeless lot, in rags, with no picturesqueness; and had a stupid, almost idiotic expression of countenance, which quite destroyed any sentiments of chivalry about them, which might have lingered in my mind from the days of Cooper's novels.

More sympathetically, Robert Louis Stevenson, on his train to San Francisco, noticed the Indians, 'over whose continent we had been steaming all these days':

Now and again at way-stations, a husband and wife and a few children, disgracefully dressed out with the sweepings of civilisation, came forth and stared upon the emigrants. The silent stoicism of their conduct, and the pathetic degradation of their appearance, would have touched any thinking creature, but my fellow-passengers danced and jested round them with a truly Cockney baseness. I was ashamed for the thing we call civilisation.

Fanny Trollope had every sympathy for the Indians, particularly as she believed they had begun to adopt some more 'civilized' white ways:

The circumstances which renders their expulsion from their own, their native lands, so peculiarly lamentable, is, that they were yielding rapidly to the force of example; their lives were no longer those of wandering hunters, but they were becoming agriculturists, and the tyrannical arm of brutal power has not now driven them, as formerly, only from their hunting grounds, their favourite springs, and the sacred bones of their fathers, but it has chased them from the dwellings their advancing knowledge had taught them to make comfortable; from the newly-ploughed fields of their pride; and from the crops their sweat had watered. And for what? to add some thousand acres of territory to the half-peopled wilderness which borders them.

Another visiting Englishwoman took up the defence of the Indians, even in their supposedly most 'savage' practices:

A war party of Indians, perhaps two or three hundred, (and that is a very large number), dance their war dance, go out and burn a village, and bring back twenty or thirty scalps. *They* are savages and heathens. We Europeans fight a battle, leave fifty thousand dead or dying by inches on the field, and a hundred thousand to mourn them, desolate; but *we* are civilised and Christians . . . One scalps his enemy, the other rips him open with a sabre; one smashes his brains with a tomahawk, and the other blows him to atoms with a cannon-ball: and to me, femininely speaking, there is not a needle's point difference between the one and the other. If war be unchristian and barbarous, then war as a *science* is more absurd, unnatural, unchristian, than war as a passion.

ANNA BROWNELL JAMESON

There was certainly a curiosity about the more blood-thirsty practices of Indians. Settlers sometimes found themselves enjoying good relations with their neighbouring tribe, while the tribe itself was in deadly conflict with those on its borders. Any stories about massacres or scalping – preferably reported at second- or third-hand – added a welcome element of spice to any account of North American experiences.

Richard Francis Burton, on his way to visit the Mormons of Salt Lake City, Utah, in 1860, reported on the scalping practices of the Sioux Indians whose territory he crossed. He learned that scalping was essentially the removal of a trophy from one's enemy, consisting of an area of skin and a long piece of hair (the scalp-lock) from the front of the head. Prudent white travellers made sure they had had their heads shaved in this area before crossing known Indian country, so as to be poor subjects for the operation. Burton tried to persuade a member of the Sioux tribe to demonstrate the moves, but the Indian, to whom scalping was a serious, solemn ritual, refused. Burton was still able to offer his readers some authentic details:

> The operator sits on the ground, places his feet against the subject's shoulders by way of leverage, and holding the scalp-lock with both hands he applies a strain which soon brings off the spoils with a sound which, I am told, is not unlike a 'flop'.
>
> A few cunning men have surprised their adversaries with wigs. The operation of scalping must be exceedingly painful . . . many instances, however, are known of men and even women recovering from it.

The difficulties created for native Indians by the arrival of white people were, in reality, much less glamorous and colourful than could be suggested by any picture of whooping, tomahawk-swinging bands of men on horseback in search of scalps. The Indians were deprived of their land, and given disease and alcohol in its place. Captain Marryat concluded that alcohol had a more devastating effect on the Indians than any war with the whites. He met the daughter of a great Mohican chief, Red Jacket, already dead, and heard about his enslavement to drink:

> When Red Jacket was sober he was the proudest chief that ever walked, and never would communicate even with the highest of the American authorities but through his interpreter; but when intoxicated he would speak English and French fluently, and then the proud Indian warrior, the most eloquent of his race, the last chief of the six nations, would demean himself by begging for a sixpence to buy more rum.

Marryat also complained that a more direct injustice was practiced on the Indians by the American government, who 'bought' land from them for a low price, and then sold it to settlers, making a huge profit on the exchange: 'well may the Indians be said, like Esau, to part with their birthright for a mess of pottage; but, in truth, they are *compelled* to sell – the purchase-money being a mere subterfuge, by which it may appear as if their lands were not wrested from them.' This theme was taken up by other writers:

> The Americans will never solve the Indian problem till the Indian is extinct. They have treated them after a fashion which has intensified their treachery and 'devilry' as enemies, and as friends reduces them to a degraded pauperism, devoid of the very first elements of civilisation . . . 'To get rid of the Injuns' is the phrase used everywhere. Even their

'The red man . . . never appears to advantage as a resident among civilised men.'
SUSANNA MOODIE

'reservations' do not escape seizure practically; for if gold 'breaks out' on them they are 'rushed'; and their possessors are either compelled to accept land farther west or are shot off and driven off.

ISABELLA BIRD

However Mr Munroe and others may attempt to philosophize upon the benefits which arise from uncivilized man's making way before a more 'dense population,' the admitted fact is, that Americans are making continued encroachments upon the aboriginal inhabitants, either under the semblance of treaties, or by direct warfare, produced, as the present one is said to have been, by designed aggressions, and aggravating insults on the part of the people of the United States.

Henry Bradshaw Fearon

Some British writers, particularly those who had connections in influential circles in Washington, were left with a different impression. Lady Theodora Guest based her views on what she had seen through the windows of her private train as it made its whistle-stop tour of the continent:

> The United States government is very fair towards them, and does what can be done to educate and maintain them; but restricts them, wisely, to certain reservations, where they are supplied with food, and all they need . . . Happily, I think, the tribes are dying out from illnesses and epidemics, and this is surely not to be regretted.

This shocking sentiment, seldom recorded so explicitly, would have outraged British travellers who knew or talked to Indians. The Indian chief whom Dickens met on a steamboat summed up the politics astutely, and tempered his genuine goodwill towards Dickens with an awareness of the turbulent waters across which such personal bridges were built:

> There were but twenty thousand of the Choctaws left, he said, and their number was decreasing every day. A few of his brother chiefs had been obliged to become civilised, and to make themselves acquainted with what the whites knew, for it was their only chance of existence. But there were not many; and the rest were as they always had been. He dwelt on this: and said several times that unless they tried to assimilate themselves to their conquerors, they must be swept away before the strides of civilised society.
>
> When we shook hands at parting, I told him he must come to England, as he longed to see the land so much: that I should hope to see him there one day: and that I could promise him he would be well received and kindly treated. He was evidently pleased by this assurance, though he rejoined with a good-humoured smile and an arch shake of his head, that the English used to be very fond of the Red Men when they wanted their help, but had not cared much for them since.

CHAPTER NINE
SLAVES

No traveller in the United States who desires to record his free, unbiased opinions can give the go-by to the question of slavery.

CHARLES MACKAY

The presence of slavery in the southern states was a magnet for European travellers: their attempts to see the system for themselves were reported in tones which combined genuine amazement at finding men, women and children living in captivity, with a lurid curiosity about the slaves' lives and conditions.

The experience began with one's first encounter with a slave. For Fanny Trollope, the moment came soon after her arrival in North America, during a walk through the wealthy residential streets of New Orleans. Mrs Trollope wanted to examine some of the vegetables growing in the garden of a particular house:

A young Negress was employed on the steps of the house; that she was a slave made her an object of interest to us. She was the first slave we had ever spoken to, and I believe we all felt that we could hardly address her with sufficient gentleness. She little dreamed, poor girl, what deep sympathy she excited; she answered us civilly and gaily, and seemed amused at our fancying there was something unusual in red pepper pods; she gave us several of them, and I felt fearful lest a hard mistress might blame her for it . . . I left England with feelings so strongly opposed to slavery, that it was not without pain I witnessed its effects around me. At the sight of every Negro man, woman and child that passed, my fancy wove some little romance of misery, as belonging to each of them; since I have known more on the subject, and become better acquainted with their real situation in America, I have often smiled at recalling what I then felt.

Others also recorded their first awareness of being in a slave state:

We stopped to dine at Baltimore, and being now in Maryland, were waited on, for the first time, by slaves. The sensation of exacting any service from human creatures who are bought and sold, and being, for the time, a party as it were to their condition, is not an enviable

'If laughter indicates happiness, I have never seen people so happy as the domestic negroes in the towns.'
WILLIAM MAKEPEACE THACKERAY

one. The institution exists, perhaps, in its least repulsive and most mitigated form in such a town as this; but it *is* slavery; and though I was, with respect to it, an innocent man, its presence filled me with a sense of shame and self-reproach.

CHARLES DICKENS

Here I encountered the first slaves I ever saw, and the sight of them in no way tended to alter my previous opinions upon this subject. They were poorly clothed; looked horribly dirty, and had a lazy recklessness in their air and manner as they sauntered along, which naturally belongs to creatures without one of the responsibilities which are the honorable burden of rational humanity.

FANNY KEMBLE

Arriving at Portsmouth, Virginia, in 1838, Fanny Kemble took a close look at the slaves because her husband was an American slave-owner, and she was on her way to visit his estates for the first time. She had been a successful English actress on tour in America when she met and married Pierce Butler, a young man from Philadelphia who was heir to his father's plantations in Georgia, and the ownership of seven hundred slaves. 'When I married Mr Butler I knew nothing of these dreadful possessions of his', she wrote in her journal. Kemble gave up the stage, and four years after marrying, at her own insistence, visited her husband's cotton and rice plantations. The resulting journal described daily life on the estate. It told how the slaves suffered under a harsh rule, but still maintained a disconcerting respect, even a cheerful affection, for their owners.

As the master's wife, Kemble inspected the plantation with a thoroughness other British writers visiting other slave estates were denied. One day she found the infirmary, a wooden building of four rooms:

> Here lay women expecting every hour the terrors and agonies of childbirth, others who had just brought their doomed offspring into the world, others who were groaning over the anguish and bitter disappointment of miscarriages – here lay some burning with fever, others chilled with cold and aching with rheumatism, upon the hard, cold ground, the draughts and dampness of the atmosphere increasing their sufferings, and dirt, noise, and stench, and every aggravation of which sickness is capable, combined in their condition – here they lay like brute beasts, absorbed in physical suffering . . . I stood in the midst of them, perfectly unable to speak, the tears pouring from my eyes at this sad spectacle of their misery, myself and my emotion alike strange and incomprehensible to them.

Kemble also visited the filthy huts in which slave families lived, and encouraged the inhabitants to clean them up and stop the chickens and ducks wandering in and out. Her accounts contrast sharply with those of visitors escorted round estates as guests of the owners. Anthony Trollope was won over by what he saw:

> I went into some of their cottages on the estate which I visited, and was not in the least surprised to find them preferable in size, furniture, and all material comforts to the dwellings of most of our own agricultural labourers. Any comparison between the material comfort of a Kentucky slave and an English ditcher and delver would be preposterous. The Kentucky slave never wants for clothing fitted to the weather. He eats meat twice a day, and has three good meals; he knows no limit but his own appetite; his work is light; he has many varieties of amusement; he has instant medical assistance at all periods of necessity for himself, his wife, and his children.

Similarly, William Makepeace Thackeray, on an extensive lecture tour in 1855, reported that British complaints about American slavery had been overstated: 'I have no doubt that, at

THE WRITERS

FANNY KEMBLE (1809–93) wrote her *Journal of a Residence on a Georgian Plantation* (1863) in secret, away from the eyes of her husband, the plantation owner. When it was published many years later, the journal revealed the inner torment of the former English actress who found herself living within a system she could not neither tolerate nor change: 'The more I hear, and see, and learn, and ponder the whole of this system of slavery, the more impossible I find it to conceive how its practicers and upholders are to justify their deeds before the tribunal of their own conscience or God's law.'

no period of time, since wool first grew on human skulls, negroes have never been so well off as those now in America.'

Both these writers denied that their observations supported slavery ('I would not have it supposed that I conceive slavery with all these comforts to be equal to freedom without them,' said Anthony Trollope; 'this does not make slavery right: but – I can't mend it, and so leave it,' said Thackeray) but they were clearly aware that what they had written required such denials. Trollope was so enthusiastic about the conditions under which the slave lived that he could talk about 'the advantages of which abolition would deprive him'.

Fanny Kemble was unimpressed by such testimonies, claiming that visitors were never shown the truth of slavery:

> It is morally impossible for any Englishman going into the Southern states, except as a *resident*, to know anything whatever of the real condition of the slave population . . . The Southerners are as anxious to hide its uglier features from any note-making observer from this side of the water as to present to his admiration and approval such as can by any possibility be made to wear the most distant approach to comeliness.

Dickens was well aware of being guided by his hosts when he toured the Southern states in 1842. In Virginia, he visited a tobacco processing plant where the slaves were allowed to sing while they worked, only a certain number at a time, and only after two in the afternoon. When a bell rang, the men left their work and crossed the street for dinner. 'I said several times that I should like to see them at their meal,' Dickens wrote, 'but as the gentleman to whom I mentioned this desire appeared to be suddenly taken rather deaf, I did not pursue the request.' The next day, at a plantation, Dickens was allowed to see the slave huts ('very crazy, wretched cabins'), but only from the outside.

One of the most confusing experiences for the liberal-minded visitor was the observation of what seemed genuine affection between slaves and their owners. The story told to Amelia Murray was typical of those with which slave-owners tried to win the sympathy of British visitors:

> One gentleman told me that he has a distant plantation, which he sometimes visits alone; at dinner-time he finds a table loaded with all kinds of delicacies, presents from the slaves. He remonstrated with an old Darkey who waited, upon the uselessness of dressing fowls, turkey, ducks, ham, & c., for one person. 'No matter, massa. When massa comes, must have good dinner on table, whether massa eat or not.'

In 1857 the journalist Charles Mackay visited the slave states, and described, as he saw it, the harmonious intimacy between slaves and their owners:

'I was not invited to enter into any of their huts. All I saw of them, was, that they were very crazy, wretched cabins, near to which groups of half-naked children basked in the sun.'

CHARLES DICKENS

Black women nurse the little white girl in her babyhood – wash her, dress her, and adorn her – take her to school in her girlhood – and share in all the joys and sorrows of her youth . . . The faithful slave, looked upon as a friend, receives the familiar and affectionate title of 'uncle' or 'aunt,' as sex may dictate. If the master or mistress be young, and the 'uncle' or 'aunt' old, the negroes exercise the right of advice, authority, and control in every thing that relates to personal comfort and domestic ease.

Sarah Mytton Maury, staying at the smart Astor House hotel in New York, asked a fellow-guest, a Georgia planter, about the chances of an uprising of slaves against their owners:

'It is perfectly preposterous,' was his reply, 'You think me safe here, in the Astor House, and so do I, but on my own plantation I am twenty times more safe than I am here. Tomorrow we leave New York to return home, and if you were to accompany us, you would see that on our return we shall be attended by whole groups of the black people; some of them will salute Mrs Dawson, all will shake hands, and I shall have a dozen or two of those little black rascals swarming upon my knees; it will be the signal for a general holiday within doors and out.

Even Fanny Kemble did not deny that slave-owners received this kind of reception at their estates. She had been the bemused recipient of the same attentions at her husband's plantations. She was repeatedly thanked by the slaves for her presence, and for providing her husband with a daughter, who would one day inherit the estate. In her journal, she remembered the slaves at the last Sunday church service before she returned north: 'their eyes never wandered from me and my child, who sat close by my knee, their little mistress, their future providence, my poor baby!'

It was this hope of future stability which explained the attitude of slaves to the owner families: the slaves were genuinely interested in the owners' well-being because that was their best guarantee that their own lives would, at least, get no worse. If the family succession ended, or the business went bankrupt, slaves would be sold, families would be split up, or a new and unpredictable regime would replace the arrangements they knew.

The owners' regard for their slaves was similarly compromised: intimacy with slaves was possible because they were invisible, as Fanny Trollope discovered:

A Virginian gentleman told me that ever since he had married, he had been accustomed to have a negro girl sleep in the same chamber with himself and his wife. I asked for what purpose this nocturnal attendance was necessary? 'Good heavens!' was the reply, 'if I wanted a glass of water during the night, what would become of me?'

Slaves were also financial assets, a form of human capital, as both they and their owners were well aware. Fanny Kemble had this fact indelicately brought to her attention by women slaves:

> A woman thinks, and not much amiss, that the more frequently she adds to the number of her master's livestock by bringing new slaves into the world, the more claims she will have upon his consideration and good will. This was perfectly evident to me from the meritorious air with which the women always made haste to inform me of the number of children they had borne, and the frequent occasions on which the older slaves would direct my attention to their children, exclaiming: 'Look, missis! little niggers for you and massa; plenty little niggers for you and little missis!'

Even the most impressionable traveller who imagined, in seeing relaxed smiles and warmth between whites and blacks, that slavery might have a benign face, would be brought back to reality by visiting a slave auction. Isabella Strange Trotter visited Ashland, Kentucky, in 1858, and inspected the slave pens in the market:

> There were about forty negroes for sale; they had within the last few days, sold about 100, who had travelled by railway chained together. Those we saw, were divided into groups, and we went through a variety of rooms in which they were domiciled, and were allowed to converse freely with them all . . . These pens give one a much more revolting idea of the institution than seeing the slaves in regular service.

Other visitors at other auctions, observed the same scenes. Their descriptions continue the story:

> By degrees more people arrived. When about fifty were present, the slaves were brought in from the neighbouring jail, where they had been confined. There were four men, and two girls. The former were immediately led behind the screen, stripped stark naked, and examined with great minuteness. Marks were criticised with the knowing air assumed by horse dealers, and pronounced to be the results of flogging, vermin, or scrofula . . . The women were more tenderly dealt with. Personal examination was confined to the hands, arms, legs, bust, and teeth. Searching questions were put respecting their age, and whether they had children. If they replied in the negative, their bosoms were generally handled in a repulsive and disgusting manner.
>
> CHARLES WELD

A girl with two little children was on the block: 'Likely girl, Amy and her two children, good cook, healthy girl, Amy - what! only seven hundred dollars for the three? that is giving 'em away! 720! 730! 735! – 740! why, gentlemen, they are worth a thousand dollars – healthy family, good washer, house servant, etc. $750.' . . . I came away very sick with the noise and the sickening moral and physical atmosphere.

BARBARA BODICHON

After witnessing scenes like this, some travellers still left the slave states with a message about how the evils of slavery had been exaggerated, or even imagined. Amelia Murray concluded:

It appears to me our benevolent intentions in England have taken a mistaken direction, and that we should bestow our compassion on the masters instead of the slaves. The former by no means enjoy the incubus with which circumstances have loaded them, and would be only too happy if they could supercede this black labour by white; but as to the negroes, they are the merriest, most contented set of people I ever saw . . . Even as to the matter of purchase and sale, it is disliked by masters; and I find compassion very much wasted upon the objects of it.

And Sarah Mytton Maury could find no moral or practical objections:

I would reside by choice in a Slave State; I like the disposition, I like the service, I like the affection of the Slave; I like the bond which exists between him and his master; the union of interests, and the companionship which death alone destroys; such intercourse is equally compatible with existing facts, and agreeable to my own views of social and domestic arrangements.

Fanny Trollope echoed these responses, claiming she was 'immediately comfortable, and at my ease' in a slave state, and even that she felt her contact with slaves was 'profitable to both parties and painful to neither'. But she was more of a politician than either of the above writers, and weighed the idea of slavery against an American doctrine, which, to some British writers, was almost as controversial:

I am very far from intending to advocate the system of slavery; I conceive it to be essentially wrong; but so far as my observation has extended, I think its influence is far less injurious to the manners and morals of the people than the fallacious ideas of equality, which are so fondly cherished by the working classes of the white population in America.

Mrs Trollope was one of many Britons to draw attention to the contradiction between the commitment to liberty in the Declaration of Independence, and the practice of slavery: 'you will see them with one hand hoisting the cap of liberty, and with the other flogging their slaves,' she noted.

Sometimes, the first-hand observation of slavery failed to clarify the moral position. Finding slave-owners to be anything less than the embodiment of evil was confusing. 'Instead of seeing my way better as I went on, I found my ideas on the intricate and formidable subject of slavery, becoming rather less clear than I fancied they had formerly been,' wrote Basil Hall: 'the different accounts which different people gave me of the actual condition of the negroes, sorely distracted every general conclusion I ventured to draw.'

But on the journey back north, the slightest distance from the reality of slavery gave many visitors the perspective they needed to come to the conclusion they desired:

> I went upon my way with a grateful heart that I was not doomed to live where slavery was, and had never had my senses blunted to its wrongs and horrors in a slave-rocked cradle.
>
> CHARLES DICKENS

> Yesterday as we rattled along in the rail, about two o'clock we came to a ploughed field, nothing particular to look at, and in it was standing a stick and (nothing particular to look at) on this stick was a white flag. That was Mason and Dixon's line that was the boundary between the Slave States and the Free, between Delaware and Pennsylvania – and though the air did not change or the land look happier as we passed and came on this side, I can tell you my feelings changed so much that it seemed to me as if everything was better, brighter, truer, at once.
>
> BARBARA BODICHON

Fanny Kemble remained resolute in her views: 'of course, of the abstract question I could judge before I came here, but I confess I had not the remotest idea how absolutely my observation of every detail of the system, as a practical iniquity, would go to confirm my opinion of its abomination.'

This view made for difficult relations with her husband, the plantation-owner. He eventually forbade his wife to draw to his attention any requests made to her by the slaves. Instead, she chronicled their forlorn experiences in her journal, kept secretly. In the plantation infirmary, there was more to be witnessed:

> I found, on entering the first ward – to use a most inapplicable term for the dark, filthy, forlorn room I have so christened – an old Negro called Friday lying on the ground. I asked what ailed him, and was told he was dying. I approached him, and perceived, from the glazed eyes and the feeble rattling breath, that he was at the point of expiring. His tattered shirt and trousers barely covered his poor body; his appearance was that of utter exhaustion from age and feebleness; he

'The evils I see here are immense, and the corrupting influence of this system so bad, so deep, that it seems almost impossible to exaggerate it.'

BARBARA BODICHON

had nothing under him but a mere handful of straw that did not cover the earth he was stretched on; and under his head, by way of pillow for his dying agony, two or three rough sticks just raising his skull a few inches from the ground. The flies were all gathering around his mouth, and not a creature was near him. There he lay – the worn-out slave, whose life had been spent in unrequited labour for me and mine, without one physical alleviation, one Christian solace, one human sympathy, to cheer him in his extremity – panting out the last breath of his wretched existence like some forsaken, overworked wearied-out beast of burden, rotting where it falls! I bent over the poor awful human creature in the supreme hour of his mortality; and while my eyes, blind with tears of unavailing pity and horror, were fixed upon him, there was a sudden quivering of the eyelids and falling of the jaw – and he was free. I stood up, and remained long lost in the imagination of the change that creature had undergone, and in the tremendous overwhelming consciousness of the deliverance God had granted the soul whose castoff vesture of decay lay at my feet. How I rejoiced for him; and how, as I turned to the wretches who were calling to me from the inner room, whence they could see me as I stood contemplating the piteous object, I wished they all were gone away with him, the delivered, the freed by death from bitter, bitter bondage.

'Every Englishman probably looks forward to the accomplishment of abolition of slavery at some future day. I feel as sure of it as I do of the final judgment. When or how it shall come I will not attempt to foretell.'
ANTHONY TROLLOPE

Fanny Kemble's marriage to Pierce Butler survived for more than a decade after her visit to Georgia, but ended in divorce, with Butler being given custody of the children. Kemble's plantation journal was published twenty-five years after it was written – any sooner would, she believed, have been an abuse of her privileges as the owner's wife. When she finally agreed to the journal being published, in 1863, she had returned to acting, Butler's estate had been sold to pay his debts, and Lincoln's Emancipation Proclamation had made the end of slavery one of the main objects of the Civil War. Two years later, the abolition of slavery was confirmed by the ratification of the Thirteenth Amendment to the United States Constitution.

CHAPTER TEN
THE DANGERS OF DEMOCRACY

Washington left America a republic, and in the short space of fifty years it has sunk into a democracy.

CAPTAIN MARRYAT

The British had their monarchy, lending stability and a certain tone to their country. Parliament made the laws, but it was the monarchy which held society in its rightful shape, a pyramid, with the king or queen at the top, the aristocracy beneath, and ladies and gentleman below them, above their servants and anyone else who had to work for a living. In America, as the British saw it, nobody knew where they were: there was an experiment under way in which political responsibility was given to ordinary people in a dangerously haphazard way. Family experience, connections or education seemed to count for nothing when it came to being elected. The Americans didn't even mind if their politicians needed money; members of congress were paid $8 a day ('positive wealth' for some, said Alexander Mackay). In Britain only gentlemen could afford to campaign for election, and sit unpaid in the House of Commons.

James Russell Lowell, the American writer, later appointed as United States minister to Great Britain, commented: 'I never blamed England for not wishing well to democracy. How should she?' His essay, called 'On a Certain Condescension in Foreigners', was described by the British poet and critic Matthew Arnold as 'rather tart'. British condescension was not limited to questions of American political leadership: the British also felt Americans lacked guidance on general matters of morality, with no established Church, and on mundane but tricky subjects such as etiquette and personal habits. When the British visited Congress, their worst fears, on all these counts, were confirmed:

Except when some remarkably good speaker has 'possession of the floor,' the members, instead of attending to what is spoken, are busied in conversation – in writing letters –

rapping the sand off the wet ink with their knuckles – rustling the countless multitude of newspapers which deluge the House – locking or unlocking their drawers – or moving up and down the avenues which divide the ranges of seats, and kicking before them, at every step, printed reports, letter covers, and other documents strewed on the floor.

BASIL HALL

Criticisms of the dress, manners, and tidiness of politicians were important, because, to British eyes, they meant, simply, that the country was not being governed by gentlemen:

Both houses are handsomely carpeted; but the state to which these carpets are reduced by the universal disregard of the spitoon with which every honourable member is accommodated, and the extraordinary improvements on the pattern which are squirted and dabbled upon it in every direction, do not admit of being described. I will merely observe, that I strongly recommend all strangers not to look at the floor; and if they happen to drop anything, though it be their purse, not to pick it up with an ungloved hand on any account.

It is somewhat remarkable too, at first, to say the least, to see so many honourable members with swelled faces; and it is scarcely less remarkable to discover that this appearance is caused by the quantity of tobacco they contrive to stow within the hollow of the cheek. It is strange enough too, to see an honourable gentleman leaning back in his tilted chair with his legs on the desk before him, shaping a convenient 'plug' with his penknife, and when it is quite ready for use, shooting the old one from his mouth, as from a pop-gun, and clapping the new one in its place.

CHARLES DICKENS

With the most earnest attention, I could only follow one or two of the orators, whose voices were peculiarly loud and clear. This made it a real labour to listen; but the extreme beauty of the chamber was of itself a reason for going again and again. It was, however, really mortifying to see this splendid hall, fitted up in so stately and sumptuous a manner, filled with men, sitting in the most unseemly attitudes, a large majority with their hats on, and nearly all, spitting to an excess that decency forbids me to describe.

The Senate-chamber is, like the Hall of Congress, a semicircle, but of very much smaller dimensions. It is most elegantly fitted up, and what is better still, the senators, generally speaking, look like gentlemen. They do not wear their hats, and the activity of youth being happily past, they do not toss their heels above their heads. I would I could add they do not spit; but, alas! 'I have an oath in heaven,' and may not write an untruth.

FANNY TROLLOPE

'Even in Winter, when Congress is sitting, Washington is melancholy; – but Washington in summer must surely be the saddest spot on earth.'

ANTHONY TROLLOPE

For all her criticisms, Mrs Trollope recorded her appreciation at being allowed to attend Congress, women being at the time, as she said, 'rigorously excluded' from the House of Commons. This was not the only way in which British visitors could report on American politics with first-hand accounts: many also met the President. The Presidency was a relatively informal institution, the President often travelling by public steamboat or train, and being open to visits when in Washington. Fanny Trollope's husband booked himself onto a boat from Cincinnati to Pittsburgh in 1829, deliberately hoping to meet a fellow-passenger, the newly-elected General Jackson. Mrs Trollope says her husband 'conversed a good deal' with the President and was 'pleased by his conversation and manners'.

Thomas Hamilton achieved greater intimacy during a half-hour private audience with General Jackson in Washington. Hamilton found him 'a very decent-looking old gentleman, something like a country minister in Scotland, and kind, though somewhat vulgar in manner'. The President, said Hamilton, 'told me he was always at home of an evening, and would be glad to see me when I chose to drop in'. The next day Hamilton received a dinner invitation from the President, but turned it down because he was already busy; another evening he took up the President's offer to 'drop in':

> The President was gone up stairs with a headache. I sent up my card with my respects, and he came down. The conversation for the first quarter of an hour was about the state of his bowels, the failure of calomel, the success of salts, & c. & c. We then got on European politics, on which all he said was commonplace enough.

Hamilton found General Jackson's openness remarkable: 'nothing is more striking to an European than the utter absence, in this country, of *official reserve*.'

The same surprise was felt by the Methodist minister James Dixon, whose introduction to President Polk in 1848 was effected by turning up at the White House with some colleagues, who sent in a message, requesting a meeting with the President. An immediate invitation was returned, and Dixon found President Polk 'grave, thoughtful, meditative, and slow and measured in his speech'. What struck him most was the informality: 'here, then, we were, four Methodist preachers, and one merchant, snugly ensconced in a government office, a sort of counting-house, with President Polk, one of the greatest men, by position, in the world!' Dixon could not decide whether he approved of this style:

> Truly this American republicanism must either be considered as a great retrogression into the ages of social simplicity, when shepherds and farmers left their flocks and ploughs to command armies and govern states, and then returned to their avocations; or else it must be considered as a vast stretch into the future, the anticipation of something to come, the model of a perfectly new order of things.

Similarly, Dickens met President Tyler at the White House ('his manner was remarkably unaffected, gentlemanly and agreeable'), and was invited to dinner (but again was unable to accept the invitation because of prior arrangements). Amelia Murray met President Pierce ('a quiet-looking, pale, gentlemanly man'), Henry Bradshaw Fearon attended one of President Monroe's weekly drawing-rooms, reporting 'there is little or no difficulty in getting introduced on these occasions'; he found the President 'a very plain, practical man of business'. And Charles Weld introduced himself to the President: 'I accompanied a gentleman to the White House, and after the mere formality of sending in my card, was admitted to the presence of General Franklin Pierce.'

For all this Presidential attention, British visitors felt, somewhat hypocritically, that the Presidency was too accessible. Captain Marryat noted changes introduced by President Van Buren, who followed General Jackson, to restrict entry to Presidential parties, and stop 'the mobocracy' from attending:

'The "White House" is singularly simple and unpretending in its interior decoration, certainly it cannot fairly be termed a palace, and it is scarcely equal to a tolerably well-appointed private abode.'

CLARA BROMLEY

The police are now stationed at the door, to prevent the intrusion of any improper person. A few years ago, a fellow would drive his cart, or hackney coach, up to the door, walk into the saloon in all his dirt, and force his way to the President, that he might shake him by the one hand while he flourished his whip in the other. The revolting scenes which took place when refreshments were handed round, the injury done to the furniture, and the disgust of the ladies may well be imagined. Mr. Van Buren deserves great credit for this step.

Mrs Trollope's husband, on his steamboat with General Jackson, had witnessed the kind of behaviour Marryat was complaining about. Mrs Trollope relayed her husband's report that he was 'deeply disgusted' with the 'brutal familiarity' suffered by the General, a recent widower, and gave the following example:

I was at his elbow when a greasy fellow accosted him thus:-

'General Jackson, I guess?'

The General bowed assent.

'Why they told me you was dead.'

'No! Providence has hitherto preserved my life.'

'And is your wife alive too?'

The General, apparently much hurt, signified the contrary, upon which the courtier concluded his harangue, by saying: 'Aye, I thought it was the one or the t'other of ye.'

This kind of familiarity was more than a question of etiquette or security; it was the expression of a pervasive attitude held by both politicians and people, one that many British travellers could not stomach. Captain Marryat might have been commenting on poor General Jackson's encounter when he lamented: 'how different from England, and the settled nations of the Old World, where it may be said that everything and everybody is comparatively speaking in his place!'

Marryat's whole expedition to the States was to discover 'what were the effects of a democratic form of government and climate' upon the American people. He approved of George Washington's infant republic, 'regulated by a small body of men', but distinguished it from what had developed half a century later. Originally, he explained, the most talented in the country were selected to act 'for the benefit of the people . . . without any shackle or pledge being enforced'. Today, he found that 'those selected by the people to represent them are not only bound by pledges previous to their election, but ordered by the mass how to vote after their election.' Democracy had become a tyranny of the majority; public opinion was an all-powerful force with which no individual, elected or not, wanted to be seen to disagree. Marryat claimed that the current equivalent of Washington's 'small body of men' no longer exposed themselves to the humiliation of democratic politics:

No high-minded consistent man will now offer himself . . . The scum is uppermost . . . The prudent, the enlightened, the wise, and the good have all retired into the shade, preferring to pass a life of quiet retirement, rather than submit to the insolence and dictation of the mob.

Marryat was not alone in this line of criticism. Edward Sullivan, on a Mississippi steamer, was warned his life could be in danger if he was overheard supporting the abolition of slavery; he concluded that all the talk of American liberty was just talk: '*public opinion*, that hundred-headed hydra, and the tyranny of the majority, that most intolerant and bigoted of all tyrannies, rules America with a rod of iron.'

Even Bertrand Russell, the English philosopher, who visited America with his American wife, Alys Pearsall Smith, in 1896, complained about public opinion:

> Individual Americans are delightful: but whether from lack of courage or from decentralization, they do not form a society of frank people, and all in turn complain that they would be universally cut if they ever spoke their minds.

The Russells had a taste of this treatment when Alys caused a scandal at one college they were visiting by advocating 'free love' to a group of women she was addressing: Russell says they were 'practically hounded out' of the college.

According to the British, this dictatorship of the majority extended into all areas of life. In the Church, a congregation could dismiss a minister with which it was displeased; in schools a 'democratic' interpretation of history was taught; and the press played to the lowest appetites of its readers.

On all these subjects, British writers' opinions were undoubtedly affected by the incidental events of their travels. Lofty political analysis might often have been the result of an irritating incident, or an encounter with an unhelpful individual. Captain Marryat's critical report on the press was coloured by a bitter dispute that arose when American newspapers picked up on undiplomatic remarks he made about a current conflict between Canada and the United States. Anthony Trollope's gaudy political colours ('I dislike universal suffrage; I dislike vote by ballot; I dislike above all things the tyranny of democracy') resurfaced in a more practical arena. In this case, as in many others, the theory of equality, so ringingly vivid from the Declaration of Independence, had consequences the British traveller found unacceptable. Trollope was discussing service on the American railways:

> The one grand fault is that they admit but one class . . . If a first-class railway carriage should be held as offensive, so should a first-class house, or a first-class horse, or a first-class dinner. But first-class houses, first-class horses, and first-class dinners are very rife in America . . . The railways are afraid to put themselves at variance with the general feeling of the people. If so the railways may be right. But then, on the other hand, the general feeling of the people must in such a case be wrong.

Democracy was based on equality, and expressions of equality irked the British. One field in particular was a constant source of complaint: in domestic life, ideas of equality had a troublesome effect on the servants. Frances Wright described the dangerous influence of American ideas on newly-arrived servants from Europe, who had, until then, known their place:

'If a first-class railway carriage should be held as offensive, so should a first-class house, or a first-class horse, or a first-class dinner . . . The railways are afraid to put themselves at variance with the general feeling of the people. If so the railways may be right. But then, on the other hand, the general feeling of the people must in such a case be wrong.'

ANTHONY TROLLOPE

You will easily conceive how an uneducated mind is likely to misconstrue the nature of that equality which a democracy imparts to all men . . . Those just released from the aristocracies of Europe, finding themselves in a country where all men are placed by the laws on an exact level, conceive, naturally enough, that they are transformed from the servants of their employer into his companions, and at one and the same moment lay aside obsequiousness and array themselves in insolence.

The amateur actor Captain Horton Rhys, travelling with his acting companion Lucille, had a typical encounter in a hotel in Boston:

Lucille on going to her room in the course of our first evening, rang for some one to light the gas, and after some half-dozen applications to the bell-pull was honoured with the presence of a female. I happened to enter the room at the same time, as the young lady's delay was annoying to my appetite, and the following strange colloquy ensued:–

'Please, light the gas for me.'

'Guess I'm not your chamber-gal.'

Hearing her saucy reply, and feeling rather '*riled*' thereat, I roared in her ear, 'What the devil are you, then?'

With a look of supreme contempt, she answered, as she *seated herself in a chair*, 'I'm a housekeeper, I am!'

To which Lucille said, 'Then will you be kind enough to send some one to me?'

'Yon's the bell. Guess you're near'st it; but I don't mind if I do it, this time.'

Other travellers reported similar clashes at hotels:

At night we had another sample of their *equality* . . . On reaching our bed-room we found darkness instead of the gas we expected, and we had omitted to provide or indeed think of bringing a light with us. We rang the bells and asked for a candle, when our waiter, an urchin apparently not more than thirteen or fourteen, after putting his arms akimbo and *spitting* on the floor, told us he 'guessed we might fetch one for ourselves, as we ought to have brought one with us.'

CLARA BROMLEY

Mrs E.H. Carbutt, on tour with her husband in 1888, recorded an incident at a smart New York hotel:

Our linen had returned from the laundress, and an important piece was missing, so Edward went to the office and asked the clerk to make enquiry. 'You must have counted wrong,' said the clerk; 'nobody wants your things.'

According to British observers, employers in cities who demanded servility from their servants were soon in search of new ones. But ideas of equality were just as strongly held in the outposts of society, and ignored the border into Canada. British settlers in the backwoods found themselves in great difficulties, as Thomas Need reported of a couple he visited:

The lady spoke feelingly of the privations and hardships she had endured in the first years of her exile: some of which, though softened by habit and better circumstances, still remained; one grievance she particularly dwelt upon, was the difficulty of procuring respectable servants, unless she would consent to treat them as equals, and admit them to sit at table with her husband and children; at the time of our visit, she was combining in her own person all the domestic offices, and I believe retired from the dining table to wash up the dishes and boil the tea kettle.

Need's fellow-settler John Langton, who built a farm for himself and his family in the middle of the Ontario forest, commented: 'the art of managing servants is perhaps the most important one a new settler has to learn.' With so many skills required even to survive in his new home, such a conclusion seems unlikely, but Langton explained:

The working classes here naturally feel an independence which you do not find at home, and which, if you give way as some do, will soon lead them to consider themselves your equals; others again, by endeavouring to keep them under as they call it, only give rise to insolence and make themselves cordially hated. But I have never seen any yet who by a quiet reserve of manner cannot be kept respectful. At particular moments and with particular characters you may unbend occasionally and thereby make yourself liked without losing any authority.

Langton's sister Anne and the other ladies of the household were often forced to help the servants in busy times, which, Anne remembered, was almost unheard of back in England. Once, when the family had dismissed a servant from their English home, the woman had insolently made reference to the Langtons having made their own beds, as they had on rare occasions. In Canada, Anne noted, participation in domestic activities was expected, even in the smartest families:

This summer, when our bustling household made a little help from the ladies often necessary, I used to be amused at myself going so composedly about my duties at the cooking-stove, in full sight of Mr. Atthill, occupied in the joiner's shop. One would feel shocked at such observation in England.

Compromises were required, but for many the theory of equality remained a myth. After twenty years in Canada, Susanna Moodie regarded herself as an adopted daughter of the country, but still maintained that 'equality of station is a dream – an error which is hourly contradicted by reality. As the world is at present constituted, such a state of things is impossible. The rich and the educated will never look upon the poor and ignorant as their equals.'

Not all British comments were as sceptical; Charles Dickens was enthusiastic about the self-respect and independent spirit of the American worker. Alexander Mackay tried to correct 'somewhat erroneous' reports about difficult American servants: at work, 'the servant is the servant, as in Europe'; differences from Britain were the result of servants knowing their situation could change, because they were 'not in the same position of absolute dependence as elsewhere'. Mackay attributed any friction on questions of servility to the strong identification of Americans with their political system: every American 'has asserted a great principle, and feels that, in attempting to prove it to be practicable, he has assumed an arduous responsibility'.

Even Anthony Trollope, for all his reservations about the service he received, acknowledged his approval of the principles behind these troublesome attitudes:

> Men in the States with horned hands and fustian coats are very often most unnecessarily insolent in asserting their independence . . . Precisely the same fault is to be found in Canada. I know well what men mean when they offend in this manner. And when I think on the subject with deliberation, at my own desk, I can not only excuse, but almost approve them . . . The blow at the moment of the stroke is very galling. I confess that I have occasionally all but broken down beneath it. But when it is thought of afterwards it admits of full excuse. No effort that a man can make is better than a true effort at independence.

Trollope must have forgotten the warning in his mother's book, on the dangers of a sentimental reinterpretation of their experiences by English travellers who had returned to the comfort of their own homes and servants. She remained unforgiving of American attitudes, and would surely have included her son's judgments, made with hindsight, along with the drawing-room opinions she pilloried:

> The theory of equality may be very daintily discussed by English gentlemen in a London drawing-room, when the servant, having placed a fresh bottle of cool wine on the table, respectfully shuts the door, and leaves them to their walnuts and their wisdom: but it will be found less palatable when it presents itself in the shape of a hard, greasy paw, and is claimed in accents that breathe less of freedom than of onions and whisky. Strong, indeed, must be the love of equality in an English breast if it can survive a tour through the Union.

CHAPTER ELEVEN
A NEW WORLD FOR WOMEN

Sweet and comely are the maidens of Devonshire; delicate and of gracious seeming those who live in the pleasant places of London . . . but the girls of America are above and beyond them all. They are clever; they can talk. Yea, it is said that they think. Certainly they have an appearance of doing so.

RUDYARD KIPLING

Among the subjects on which British travellers were most dogmatic was that of North American women. Although men too were sometimes treated with broad strokes of the pen, usually in unfavourable comparison with women ('the men in America fall far short of the women in intellectual cultural and moral refinement,' wrote Alexander Mackay), writers were more confident in their view of women, especially on the question of their appearance. Captain Marryat stated unequivocally that 'it must be acknowledged that American women are the *prettiest* in the world'. He explained:

> In the United States, where neither the excess of misery nor of luxury and refinement are known, you have, therefore, a more equal distribution of good looks, and, although you often meet with beautiful women, it is but rarely that you find one that may be termed ill-favoured. The *coup-d'oeil* is, therefore, more pleasing in America – enter society and turn your eyes in any direction, you will everywhere find cause for pleasure, although seldom any of annoyance.

Thomas Hamilton offered a detailed description of American women's characteristic looks and deportment:

> The average height is certainly lower than among my fair countrywomen; the cheek is without colour, and the figure sadly deficient in *en-bon-point*. But with all these disadvantages, I do not remember to have seen more beauty than I have met in New York. The features are generally finely moulded, and not unfrequently display a certain delightful

'American women are bright, clever, and wonderfully cosmopolitan.'

OSCAR WILDE

harmony, which reminds one of the *Belle Donne* of St Peter's and the Pincian Mount. The mouth alone is not beautiful; it rarely possesses the charm of fine teeth, and the lips want colour and fulness. The carriage of these fair Americans is neither French nor English, for they have the good sense to adopt the peculiarities of neither. They certainly do not paddle along, with the short steps and affected carriage of a Parisian belle, nor do they consider it becoming, to walk the streets with the stride of a grenadier. In short, though I may have occasionally encountered more grace, than has met my observation since my arrival in the United States, assuredly I have never seen less of external deportment, which the most rigid and fastidious critic could fairly censure.

It was also possible, according to Alexander Mackay, to describe a precise geographical distribution of female beauty. Mackay praised particularly the 'exquisitely moulded' feet of

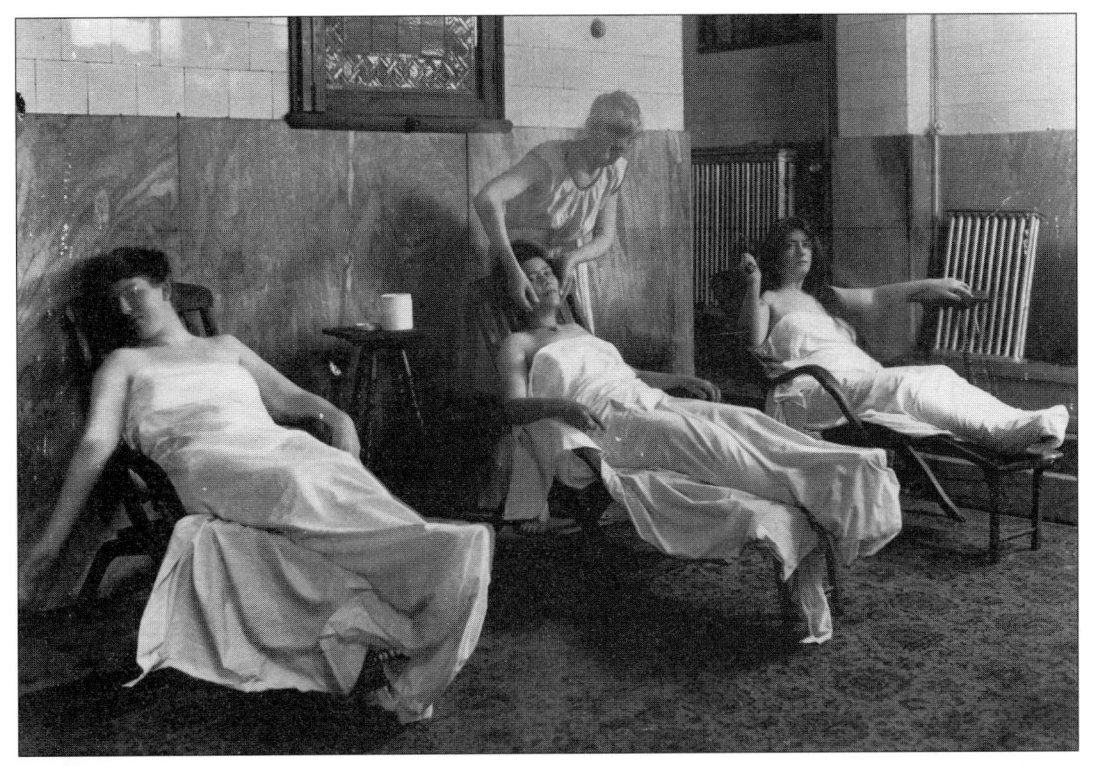

'The loveliness of American women "without paint," is an institution of itself, and I bow at its shrine.'
CAPTAIN HORTON RHYS

Maryland girls, regretted the general absence of well-rounded figures, except in 'New England, in the mountainous districts of Pennsylvania and Maryland, and in the central valley of Virginia', and noted that female beauty lasted longest in the north and north-east, 'a remark which will apply to the whole region north of the Potomac, and east of the Lakes'. Susanna Moodie summed up the situation north of the border:

> The Canadian women, while they retain the bloom and freshness of youth, are exceedingly pretty; but these charms soon fade, owing, perhaps, to the fierce extremes of the climate, or the withering effect of the dry, metallic air of stoves, and their going too early into company and being exposed, while yet children, to the noxious influence of late hours, and the sudden change from heated rooms to the cold biting, bitter winter blast.

The transience of female beauty concerned many writers. Captain Marryat reported that good looks had faded by the age of thirty. And Thomas Hamilton's enthusiasm for younger women was tempered by his description of a chilling cycle of senescence:

At one or two-and-twenty the bloom of an American lady is gone, and the more substantial materials of beauty follow soon after. At thirty the whole fabric is in decay, and nothing remains but the tradition of former conquests, and anticipations of the period, when her reign of triumph will be vicariously restored in the person of her daughter.

Female commentators came to the same conclusion; Sarah Mytton Maury blamed the customs of early schooling, early marriage, and early motherhood:

The consequences of such a pressure upon the constitution result in great bodily debility, much nervous ailment, and the premature appearance of age. I have been asked to guess the age of many ladies, and have frequently found that I over-estimated them by ten, fifteen, or twenty years.

Frances Wright observed female beauty to be 'on the wane' after the age of twenty-five. She suggested that, while not required to imitate men 'in the pursuit of the whale, the felling of the forest, or the shooting of wild turkeys', the American woman could transform herself from a 'fragile vine' to a 'vigorous tree' by taking more exercise. Others described how women relied instead on fashionable clothes and make-up to reverse the effects of age:

There are two sorts of beauty on Broadway – the beauty of Nature and the beauty of Art, and my mental exclamations of, 'What a beautiful girl!' 'What a well made-up woman!' will explain all that is necessary. Ladies no longer possessed of the bloom of youth, and with little claim to maturer charms, go in at the hare's-foot, puff, paint pot, pearl powder, and Indian ink, with Vestris-like skill, and the uninitiated are dumb-founded at their brilliance.
CAPTAIN HORTON RHYS

Fanny Trollope was at her most wounding on the subject of American female vanity, combining outspoken insult with a still more deadly tone of pity:

The ladies have strange ways of adding to their charms. They powder themselves immoderately, face, neck and arms, with pulverised starch; the effect is indescribably disagreeable by daylight, and not very favourable at any time. They are also most unhappily partial to false hair, which they wear in surprising quantities; this is the more to be lamented, as they generally have very fine hair of their own. I suspect this fashion to arise from an indolent mode of making their toilet, and from accomplished ladies' maids not being very abundant; it is less trouble to append a bunch of waving curls here, there, and every where, than to keep their native tresses in perfect order.

Though the expense of the ladies' dress greatly exceeds, in proportion to their general style of living, that of the ladies of Europe, it is very far (excepting in Philadelphia) from being in good taste. They do not consult the seasons in the colours or in the style of their costume; I have often shivered at seeing a young beauty picking her way through the snow with a pale rose-coloured bonnet, set on the very top of her head: I knew one young lady whose pretty little ear was actually frost-bitten from being thus exposed. They never wear muffs or boots, and appear extremely shocked at the sight of comfortable walking shoes and cotton stockings, even when they have to step to their sleighs over ice and snow. They walk in the middle of winter with their poor little toes pinched into a miniature slipper, incapable of excluding as much moisture as might bedew a primrose. I must say in their excuse, however, that they have, almost universally, extremely pretty feet.

Rudyard Kipling concurred on this last point, asking his reader, jocularly: 'know you that the feet of American women are like unto the feet of fairies?'

For all this discussion of appearances, writers were also interested in women's place in society. There was general agreement that North American women were given strictly chivalrous attention by men, which made it safe and relatively comfortable for them to travel alone through even the remotest parts of the continent. Frances Wright found that 'it would be impossible for women to stand in higher estimation than they do here'. She contrasted her experiences in the States with the dangers – both physical and to a woman's reputation – of travelling in England, where women saw men as 'a race of seducers rather than protectors and of masters rather than companions'. Harriet Martineau recommended America to female travellers, 'the national boast being a perfectly true one, – that a woman may travel alone from Maine to Georgia without dread of any kind of injury'. Isabella Bird's lonely travels led her to conclude that 'womanly dignity and manly respect for women are the salt of society in this wild West'. And Sarah Mytton Maury, travelling in more populous states reported: 'the solitary female ignorant of usage and of places who travels among them, has but to *look* her helplessness in order to procure assistance.'

This degree of special attention was accompanied by a rigorous separation from men. Women almost seemed to live in a different world: 'they move in different spheres, although they repose in the same bed,' said Captain Marryat of the average married couple. Even when men and women socialized, there were divisions: the New Year's day custom of visiting one's friends required the women to remain at home receiving visitors while the men rushed around the city paying calls on all the households they knew. British writers came to recognize some of these barriers in the course of their travels. Anthony Trollope discovered that although in England it is quite acceptable for a man to strike up conversation with a woman in a train, in America, it is not: 'to an American lady in a railway car I should no

'American females are even more distant and reserved in their manners than English: the sexes seem ranked as distinct races of beings, between whom social converse is rarely to be held.'

HENRY BRADSHAW FEARON

more think of speaking than I should to an unknown female in the next pew to me at a London church.' On other occasions, he found, the rules were more obvious, though just as unwelcome:

> There are ladies' doors at hotels, and ladies' drawing-rooms, ladies' sides on the ferry-boats, ladies' windows at the post office . . . At every turn it is necessary to make separate provision for ladies.

Whether, for all this, women were better or worse off, was a subject of debate. Trollope was a traditionalist, wanting to keep women out of work and politics. He believed that if women were allowed to vote alongside men, war between the sexes would break out; instead, he suggested facetiously that if women were to have political power, 'let them have it all to themselves for a season'. On the lot of women in America, he concluded, 'I think they have a "good time". I make them my compliments on their sagacity, intelligence, and attractions, but I utterly refuse to them any sympathy for supposed wrongs.'

Others were also convinced that American women would not take to politics: Tyrone Power reported that he 'never found one amongst them who thought about talking politics, unless it was with some snob who was too stupid to talk any nonsense less dull'. And Thomas Hamilton felt that women were by nature unsuited to the American system:

> No woman, conscious of attraction, was ever a republican in her heart. Beauty is essentially despotic – it uniformly asserts its power, and never yet consented to a surrender of privilege. I have certainly heard it maintained in the United States, that all men were equal, but never did I hear that assertion from the lips of a lady. On the contrary, the latter is always conscious of the full extent of her claims to preference and admiration, and is never satisfied till she feels them to be acknowledged . . . It is vain, therefore, to talk of female republicans; there exists, and can exist, no such being.

British writers listened to female conversation in society, and concluded that women were preoccupied with trivial matters. Oscar Wilde found that, in style if not content, the chatter of young American girls exerted a hypnotic fascination over his fellow-countrymen:

> If a stolid young Englishman is fortunate enough to be introduced to them he is amazed at their extraordinary vivacity, their electric quickness of repartee, their inexhaustible store of curious catchwords. He never really understands them, for their thoughts flutter about with the sweet irresponsibility of butterflies; but he is pleased and amused and feels as if he were in an aviary.

Mentally as well as physically, women seemed to occupy a different world from men: they were 'little oases of pretty unreasonableness in a vast desert of practical common sense', wrote Wilde. Some reports of women's conversation, by both men and women writers, supported him. Fanny Trollope described evening parties at Cincinnati:

> The gentlemen spit, talk of elections and the price of produce, and spit again. The ladies look at each other's dresses til they know every pin by heart; talk of Parson Somebody's last sermon on the day of judgment, on Dr. T'otherbody's new pills for dyspepsia, till the 'tea' is announced, when they all console themselves together for whatever they may have suffered in keeping awake, by taking tea, coffee, hot cake and custard, hoe cake, johny cake, waffle cake, and dodger cake.

Susanna Moodie reported that Canadian women in society seldom discussed anything except 'their own dress, or that of their neighbours, their houses, furniture, and servants, sometimes interlarded with a little harmless gossip, which, however, tells keenly upon the characters of their dear friends'. Alexander Mackay blamed the frivolity of female conversation on the dominance of young women over their mothers. It was the daughters who arranged the social events, and greeted the guests, while their mothers supervized the food from another part of the house: 'the absent mamma has her health frequently inquired for, but nobody ever thinks of wondering that she is not present.' As a result, said Mackay, rational discussion was rare: 'dreary commonplaces, jokes, and vapid compliments, form the staple of conversation, all which is attended by a never-ceasing accompaniment of laughter, which is frequently too boisterous for all tastes.'

Not all observers accepted that American women were only suited to the role of chattering passengers in society, being handed in and out of railway cars by rough but courteous men. Even Alexander Mackay thought that American women had more 'intellectual culture and moral refinement' than men, and that it was within their power to raise the general standards of society: 'if the better educated and the more intellectual class of women in America would play a more prominent part than they do in the social circles of their country, the happiest results would accrue.' Captain Marryat asserted that American women were both physically and morally of a 'higher standard' than men, and that most husbands had wives who were 'much too good for them'. He attributed the contrast to the dogged quest for money in which American men were engaged all their lives; at home, their wives were 'domestic slaves', yet had time to 'improve their minds':

All the men in America are busy; their whole time is engrossed by their accumulation of money; they breakfast early and repair to their stores or counting-houses; the majority of them do not go home to dinner, but eat at the nearest tavern or oyster-cellar, for they generally live at a considerable distance from the business part of the town, and time is too precious to be thrown away. It would be supposed that they would be home to an early tea; many are, but the majority are not. After fagging, they require recreation, and the recreations of most Americans are politics and news, besides the chance of doing a little more business, all of which, with drink, are to be obtained at the bars of the principal commercial hotels in the city. The consequence is that the major portion of them come home late, tired, and go to bed; early the next morning they are off to their business again. Here it is evident that the women do not have much of their husband's society; nor do I consider this arising from any want of inclination on the part of the husbands, as there is an absolute necessity that they should work as hard as others if they wish to do well, and what one does, the other must do. Even frequenting the bar is almost a necessity, for it is there that they obtain all the information of the day. But the result is that the married women are

'American girls are pretty and charming – little oases of pretty unreasonableness in a vast desert of practical common sense.'

OSCAR WILDE

left alone; their husbands are not their companions, and if they could be, still the majority of the husbands would not be suitable companions.

Marryat deemed these arrangements unavoidable, but censured American men for not valuing their wives, 'who have not half the influence which wives have in England or one quarter that legitimate influence to which they are entitled'. With their rightful influence, Marryat proclaimed, American women 'might save their country by checking the tide of vice and immorality, and raising the men to their own standard'.

The separation between men and women was greatest in the expanding towns and cities. In the smaller frontier settlements, where each family, often newly emigrated, was building its own home and farm, marriage was a more balanced working partnership, as Catherine Parr Traill reported:

Every young woman is prized in this country according to her usefulness; and a thriving young settler will rather marry a clever, industrious girl, who has the reputation for being a good spinner and knitter, than one who has nothing but a pretty face to recommend her. This is as it should be; and I would bid the young daughters of the emigrant to bear the fact in mind, if they wish to become the wives of steady young men, and wish to prosper in the world.

Only when new settlers achieved a little prosperity, did men and women slip into their different worlds, the men away from home, working every hour of the day, the women caught in narrow social and domestic lives, as Anne Langton described from her own experience:

As long as the lady is necessarily the most active member of her household she keeps her ground from her utility; but when the state of semi-civilisation arrives, and the delicacies of the table, and the elegancies of her person become her chief concern and pride, then she must fall, and must be contented to be looked upon as belonging merely to the decorative department of the establishment and valued accordingly.

A more optimistic view of the contribution of women came from Isabella Bird, travelling in the least developed parts of the west. There, she said, women could influence male society by being true to their best instincts:

I have seen a great deal of the roughest class of men both on sea and land during the last two years, and the more important I think the 'mission' of every quiet, refined, self-respecting woman – the more mistaken I think those who would forfeit it by noisy self-assertion, masculinity, or fastness. In all this wild West the influence of woman is second only in its benefits to the influence of religion, and where the last unhappily does not exist the first continually exerts its restraining power.

CHAPTER TWELVE

A Gazetteer of Eastern Advancement

When Mrs Trollope's party first saw the impressive Capitol in Washington, she noted that 'none of us, I believe, expected to see so imposing a structure on that side of the Atlantic'. British travellers often arrived in America not sure whether to expect to find huge, established cities, or primitive settlements under construction. Both were to be seen, and each created their own kind of surprise for the visitor.

The oldest cities were in the east, whether in the United States or Canada, and offered the British a relatively comfortable and familiar introduction to the continent before any excursions to more remote areas. In each country, there were several large eastern cities which most travellers included in their tours, and later described for their readers.

THE UNITED STATES

New York gave many Europeans their first taste of North America; its architectural grandeur and social confidence defied visitors not to be impressed. Then, as now, arriving in New York woke every traveller from the languor of the journey. In the last century, the city already offered a wealth of character and incident against which the visitor's expectations could be tested. Robert Louis Stevenson was confronted with its still-familiar reputation before he arrived:

As we drew near to New York I was at first amused, and then somewhat staggered, by the cautious and the grisly tales that went the round. You would have thought we were to land upon a cannibal island. You must speak to no one in the streets, as they would not leave you till you were rooked and beaten. You must enter a hotel with military precautions; for the least you had to apprehend was to awake the next morning without money or baggage, or necessary raiment, a lone forked radish in a bed; and if the worst befell, you would instantly and mysteriously disappear from the ranks of mankind.

Along with the dangers ('New York is not a city where either life or property is very secure,' wrote Charles Mackay), New York had a unique scale and energy. It inspired Mrs Trollope with an uncharacteristic lyricism:

We seemed to enter the harbour of New York upon waves of liquid gold, and as we darted past the green isles which rise from its bosoms, like guardian sentinels of the fair city, the setting sun stretched his horizontal beams farther and farther at each moment, as if to point out to us some new glory in the landscape.

New York, indeed, appeared to us, even when we saw it by a soberer light, a lovely and noble city. Situated on an island, which I think it will one day cover, it rises, like Venice, from the sea, and like that fairest of cities in the days of her glory, receives into its lap tribute of all the riches of the earth . . . Were all America like this fair city, and all, no, only a small proportion of its population like the friends we left there, I should say, that the land was the fairest in the world.

In 1861 Mrs Trollope's son Anthony was similarly effusive, even within his precise geographical account of New York's street plan:

First Street runs across the Avenues from water to water, and then Second Street. I will not name them all, seeing that they go up to 154th Street! They do so at least on the map, and I believe on the lamp-posts. But the houses are not yet built in order beyond 50th or 60th Street. The other hundred streets, each of two miles long, with the Avenues which are most unoccupied for four or five miles, is the ground over which the young New Yorkers are to spread themselves. I do not in the least doubt that they will occupy it all, and that 154th Street will find itself too narrow a boundary for the population.

In the last century, Broadway was the focus of smart shoppers and traders, as the city expanded north from its origins at the southern tip of Manhattan Island. Charles Dickens was entranced:

Was there ever such a sunny street as this Broadway! The pavement stones are polished with the tread of feet until they shine again; the red bricks of the houses might be yet in the dry, hot kilns; and the roofs of those omnibuses look as though, if water were poured on them, they would hiss and smoke. . . Heaven save the ladies, how they dress! We have seen more colours in these ten minutes, than we should have seen elsewhere in as many days. What various parasols! what rainbow silks and satins! what pinking of thin stockings, and pinching of thin shoes, and fluttering of ribbons and silk tassels, and display of rich cloaks with gaudy hoods and linings!

'There are eleven so-called Avenues, which descend in absolutely straight lines from the northern, and at present unsettled, extremity of the new town.'

ANTHONY TROLLOPE

Broadway was New York's Regent Street: many British visitors compared the two, some remaining patriotic to London, while others, like Captain Horton Rhys, declared without reservation that there was nothing in London to equal the magnificence of Broadway's shops. And there was another attraction with which London could not compete:

The glory of New York is the Central Park; – its glory in the mind of all New Yorkers of the present day. The first question asked of you is whether you have seen the Central Park, and the second is as to what you think of it. It does not do to say simply that it is fine, grand, beautiful, and miraculous. You must swear by cock and pie that it is more fine, more grand, more beautiful, more miraculous than anything else of the kind anywhere.

ANTHONY TROLLOPE

'The glory of New York is the Central Park; – its glory in the mind of all New Yorkers of the present day.'
ANTHONY TROLLOPE

Trollope's cynical tone may disguise a grudging admiration, but inevitably, some were less enthusiastic about the city. William Howard Russell, among other complaints, found an unwholesome metaphor for what we might call its ethnic melting-pot:

It is not to be expected, of course, that New York is a very pure city, for more than London or Paris it is the sewer of nations. It is a city of luxury also – French and Italian cooks and milliners, German and Italian musicians, high prices, extravagent tastes and dressing, money readily made, a life in hotels, bar-rooms, heavy gambling, sporting, and prize-fighting flourish here, and combine to lower the standard of the *bourgeoisie* at all events.

High prices, 'a life in hotels', fast-living – New York offered the dangers of social mobility, up or down, and a population intent on bettering itself. To the English, it could be rather distasteful:

Upon the whole, a walk through New York will disappoint an Englishman: there is, on the surface of society, a carelessness, a laziness, an unsocial indifference, which freezes the blood and disgusts the judgement.

HENRY BRADSHAW FEARON

Other, older east coast cities offered the British visitor a kind of stability which New York lacked. Boston, in particular, had a quieter, more established society in which the British felt at home. Thomas Hamilton offered a comparison between the two cities:

There is an air of gravity and solidity about Boston; and nothing gay or flashy, in the appearance of her streets, or the crowd who frequent them. New York is a young giantess, weighing twenty stone, and yet frisky withal. Boston, a matron of stayed and demure air, a little past her prime perhaps, yet showing no symptom of decay. The former is brisk, bustling, and annually outgrowing her petticoats. The latter, fat, fair, and forty, a great breeder, but turning her children out of doors, as fast as she produces them.

Some even claimed that staid Boston had an Englishness that put England itself to shame:

The Bostonians assert that they are more English than we are, that is, that they have strictly adhered to the old English customs and manners, as handed down to them previous to the revolution. That of sitting a very long while at their wine over dinner is one which they certainly adhere to, and which, I think, would be more honoured in the breach than the observance; but their hospitality is unbounded, and you do, as an Englishman, feel at home with them. I agree with the Bostonians so far, that they certainly appear to have made no change in their manners and customs for these last hundred years.

CAPTAIN MARRYAT

Charles Dickens was equally pleased with Boston, but struck a different, more American note, in describing its bright colours and advertising:

When I got into the streets upon this Sunday morning, the air was so clear, the houses were so bright and gay; the signboards were painted in such gaudy colours; the gilded letters were so very golden; the bricks were so very red, the stone was so very white, the blinds and area railings were so very green, the knobs and plates upon the street doors so marvellously bright and twinkling; and all so slight and unsubstantial in appearance – that every thoroughfare in the city looked exactly like a scene in a pantomime . . .

The city is a beautiful one, and cannot fail, I should imagine, to impress all strangers very favourably. The private dwelling-houses are, for the most part, large and elegant; the shops extremely good; and the public buildings handsome.

In Baltimore, Maryland, the British found another city which they could claim approvingly, to be pleasantly English in its culture. Its marbled homes offered the kind of luxury which the English coveted. Mrs Trollope was unstinting in her praise:

> Baltimore is in many respects a beautiful city; it has several handsome buildings, and even the private dwelling-houses have a look of magnificence, from the abundance of white marble with which many of them are adorned. The ample flights of steps, and the lofty door frames, are in most of the best houses formed of this beautiful material. Strict attention to taste and smartness . . . seems the distinguishing characteristic of the Baltimore females of all ranks.

Anthony Trollope visited Baltimore twice, and was invited on a shooting trip for canvas-back ducks, the local speciality. He politely declined, worried at the prospect of sitting alone in a hide, waiting for ducks to appear. But he admitted that gastronomically the duck 'deserves all the reputation it has acquired'. He was less taken with the other local delicacy, terrapin, which appeared as a rich soup: he complained about 'heaps of little bones' in a dish of 'no surpassing charms'. But his overall assessment of the city was affectionate:

> I found myself very happy at Baltimore. Putting aside Boston, which must, I think, be generally preferred by Englishmen to any other city in the States, I should choose Baltimore as my residence if I were called upon to live in America. I am not led to this opinion, if I know myself, solely by the canvas-back ducks; and as to the terrapins, I throw them to the winds. The madeira, which is still kept there with a reverence which I should call superstitious were it not that its free circulation among outside worshippers prohibits the just use of such a word, may have something to do with it; as may also the beauty of the women, – to some extent. Trifles do bear upon our happiness in a manner that we do not ourselves understand, and of which we are unconscious. But there was an English look about the streets and houses which I think had as much to do with it as either the wine, the women, or the ducks.

Over thirty years later, in 1895, Lady Theodora Guest also wrote warmly about the city:

> We wound down again to the station, and left it with the impression that Baltimore is a most fascinating, handsome, livable, sunny town with a southern look about it, as many darkies as whites in the streets, and a rich perfume of lilies pervading it.

'There is in Philadelphia a freedom from mere display, a relief from gaudy trappings, an evidence of solidity.'
HENRY BRADSHAW FEARON

When it came to civilized, well-ordered, established cities, the British were not always so easy to please. Philadelphia was one of the most historic cities in the United States, elegant and still proud of its Quaker origins. But the British were surprisingly consistent in their hostility. Thomas Hamilton put the complaint wittily:

There is everywhere so much appearance of real comfort, that the traveller is at first delighted with this Quaker paradise. He looks from the carriage windows prepared to see every thing *coleur de rose*. The vehicle rolls on; he praises the cleanness and neatness of the houses, and every street that presents itself seems an exact copy of those which he has left behind. In short, before he has got through half the city, he feels an unusual tendency to relaxation about the region of the mouth, which ultimately terminates in a silent but prolonged yawn.

Clara Bromley also found the geometry oppressive:

Philadelphia is generally called the 'prettiest city in the States,' on what ground I cannot imagine, unless beauty is supposed to consist in the most painfully straight lines and acute angles. Judging from the aspect of the town in this morning's perambulation, I think it probable I should expire of ennui in a week if forced to stay.

Charles Dickens imagined the city's atmosphere might produce an unwelcome transformation in his appearance:

After walking about it for an hour or two, I felt that I would have given the world for a crooked street. The collar of my coat appeared to stiffen, and the brim of my hat to expand, beneath its quakerly influence. My hair shrunk into a sleek short crop, my hands folded themselves upon my breast of their own calm accord, and thoughts of taking lodgings in Mark Lane over against the Market Place, and of making a large fortune by speculations in corn, came over me involuntarily.

While New York was criticized for its decadence, Philadelphia was found too strait-laced. Fanny Trollope longed for the chance of a little indulgence:

The great and most striking contrast between this city and those of Europe, is perceived after sunset; scarcely a sound is heard; hardly a voice or a wheel breaks the stillness. The streets are entirely dark, except where a stray lamp marks an hotel or the like; no shops are open, but those of the apothecary, and here and there a cook's shop; scarcely a step is heard, and for a note of music or the sound of mirth, I listened in vain. In leaving the theatre, which I always did before the afterpiece, I saw not a single carriage . . . Is it an European prejudice to deem that the solitary dram swallowed by the gentlemen on quitting an American theatre indicates a lower and more vicious state of manners, than do the ices so sedulously offered to the ladies on leaving a French one?

Frances Wright put the case for Philadelphia's defence:

I am not sure that the streets have not too many right angles and straight lines to be altogether pleasing to the eye, but they have so much the air of cheerfulness, cleanliness, and comfort, that it would be quite absurd to find fault with them. The side pavements are regularly washed every morning by the domestic of each house, a piece of outdoor housewifery, by the way, which must be somewhat mischievous to the ladies' thin slippers, but which adds much to the fair appearance and, I doubt not, to the good health of the city.

Along with the Quakers and the straight streets, water was the other great theme of reports from Philadelphia, a tour of the water-works being a standard feature of every tourist's visit:

Philadelphia is so admirably supplied with water from the Schuylkill water-works, that every house has it laid on from the attic to the basement; and all day long they wash windows, door, marble step, and pavements in front of the houses. Indeed, they have so much water that they can afford to be very liberal to passers-by. One minute you have a shower-bath from a Negress, who is throwing water at the windows on the first floor; and the next you have to hop over a stream across the pavement, occasioned by some black fellow who, rather than go for a broom to sweep away any small portion of dust collected before his master's door, brings out the leather hose, attached to the hydrants, as they term them here, and fizzes away with it till the stream has forced the dust into the gutter.

Of course, fire has no chance in this city. Indeed, the two elements appear to have arranged that matter between them; fire has the ascendant in New York while water reigns in Philadelphia. If a fire does break out here, the housekeepers have not the fear of being *burnt* to death before them; for the water is poured on in such torrents that the furniture is washed out of the windows, and all they have to look out for is to escape from being drowned.

CAPTAIN MARRYAT

Further down the coast, the federal capital had suffered from British attack in the war of 1812. It was still under construction to an ambitious city plan during the time of most of these accounts. While British visitors found Philadelphia too ordered, they complained that Washington was too chaotic:

Take the worst parts of the City Road and Pentonville . . . Burn the whole down; build it up again in wood and plaster; widen it a little; throw in part of St John's Wood; put green blinds outside all the private houses, with a red curtain and a white one in every window; plough up all the roads; plant a good deal of coarse turf in every place where it ought *not* to be; erect three handsome buildings in stone and marble, anywhere, but the more entirely out of everybody's way the better: call one the Post Office, and one the Treasury; make it scorching hot in the morning, and freezing cold in the afternoon, with an occasional tornado of wind and dust; leave a brick-field without the bricks, in all central places where a street may naturally be expected: and that's Washington.

It is sometimes called the City of Magnificent Distances, but it might with greater propriety be termed the City of Magnificent Intentions . . . Spacious avenues, that begin in nothing, and lead nowhere; streets, mile-long, that only want houses, roads and inhabitants;

public buildings that need but a public to be complete; and ornaments of great thoroughfares, which only lack great thoroughfares to ornament – are its leading features. One might fancy the season over, and most of the houses are gone out of town for ever with their masters.

CHARLES DICKENS

Washington's major public buildings were erected in their appointed positions, but they were not emerging from an existing city; they were to create the activity that would generate a city around them:

Everybody knows that Washington has a Capitol; but the misfortune is that the Capitol wants a city. There it stands, reminding you of a general without an army, only surrounded and followed by a parcel of ragged little dirty boys; for such is the appearance of the dirty, straggling, ill-built houses which lie at the foot of it.

CAPTAIN MARRYAT

In her generous assessment of Washington, Mrs Trollope gave the lie to her undeserved reputation for insulting all things American. Like her son, she mixed her complaints with genuine enthusiasm, not just for the achievements, but also for the hopes of America:

Our first object the next morning was to get a sight of the Capitol, and our impatience sent us forth before breakfast. The mists of morning still hung around this magnificent building when first it broke upon our view, and I am not sure that the effect produced was not the greater for this circumstance. At all events, we were struck with admiration and surprise . . .

I was delighted with the whole aspect of Washington; light, cheerful, and airy, it reminded me of our fashionable watering places. It has been laughed at by foreigners, because the original plan of the city was upon an enormous scale, and but a very small part of it has as yet been executed. But I confess I see nothing in the least degree ridiculous about it; the original design, which was as beautiful as it was extensive, has been in no way departed from, and all that has been done has been done well.

While Anthony Trollope found much to praise in the east coast cities of the United States, he reserved for the small town of Portland, Maine, a reverie which strayed into the comic:

The faces of the people tell of three regular meals of meat a day, and of digestive powers in proportion. Oh happy Portlanders, if they only knew their own good fortune! They get up early, and go to bed early. The women are comely and sturdy, able to take care of themselves without any fal-lal of chivalry; and the men are sedate, obliging, and industrious

'The total absence of all sights, sounds, or smells of commerce, adds greatly to the charm (of Washington). Instead of drays you see handsome carriages; and instead of the busy bustling hustle of men, shuffling on to a sale of "dry goods" or "prime broad stuffs," you see very well-dressed personages, lounging leisurely up and down Pennsylvania Avenue.'

FANNY TROLLOPE

. . . Probably of all modes of life that are allotted to man by his Creator, life such as this is the most happy.

As if to show that he had not completely forsaken reality, Trollope concluded with a small qualification: 'one hint, however, for improvement I must give, even to Portland! It would be well if they could make their streets of some material harder than sand.'

CANADA

Transatlantic ships bound for Quebec, Montreal and Toronto sailed up the St Lawrence. But even those heading for the United States often made their first North American port in what is now Canada. Dickens, on his way to New York, and delighted to find himself safe after a stormy voyage, ran down the gangway and 'leaped on the firm glad earth again' in Halifax, Nova Scotia. Although, he said, he would have been happy anywhere after such a trip, he carried away 'a most pleasant impression of the town, and its inhabitants'.

The other Canadian ports were also the scene of many arrivals, often of emigrant ships, landing their passengers in an unknown country, sick, poor, and confused, but elated to have reached their new home. Susanna Moodie recorded her memories of arriving in Canada for the first time:

We cast anchor before Quebec. What a scene! – Can the world produce such another? . . . Regardless of the eager crowds around me, I leant upon the side of the vessel and cried like a child – not tears of sorrow, but a gush from the heart of pure and unalloyed delight. I heard not the many voices murmuring in my ears – I saw not the anxious beings that thronged our narrow deck – my soul at that moment was alone with God. The shadow of His glory rested visibly on the stupendous objects that composed that magnificent scene.

Canadians, rejoice in your beautiful city! Rejoice and be worthy of her – for few, very few, of the sons of men can point to such a spot as Quebec – and exclaim, 'She is ours! – God gave her to us, in her beauty and strength!'

Those visiting Quebec as tourists appreciated its winding French streets. Even in 1853 there were signs of new buildings superceding the quaint and the old:

Quebec, the old part of it at least, is most irregularly built; the houses sometimes, when seen from a little distance, give the idea of being piled one upon the top of another; but this very peculiarity renders it far more picturesque than the newer and more irreproachably precise towns we have travelled through in the States.

CLARA BROMLEY

Charles Dickens, who travelled north to Quebec, overland from New York, loved the drama of its location:

The impression made upon the visitor by this Gibraltar of America: its giddy heights; its citadel suspended, as it were, in the air; its picturesque steep streets and frowning gateways; and the splendid views which burst upon the eye at every turn: is at once unique and lasting. It is a place not to be forgotten or mixed up in the mind with other places, or altered for a moment in the crowd of scenes a traveller can recall.

> 'In the afternoon I re-crossed the channel and surveyed Montreal, which has an air completely French. The streets are irregular, narrow, ill-paved, and moreover rejoice universally in a fishy savour in no way detracting from their Gallic characteristics.'
> TYRONE POWER

Kipling, too, stressed the city's uniqueness, claiming that Quebec 'ranks by herself as one of those Mother-cities of whom none can say "This reminds me"'.

The other large French-speaking city in Canada, Montreal, provoked differing reactions from visitors, who longed for a little urban civilization after a tough journey, and emigrants, who looked forward to settling on their own plot of land in the backwoods. Frances Wright was one of the former:

> It is a pleasant relief to the eye, tired with the contemplation of dreary forests and wide watery wastes, when the fair seigniority of Montreal suddenly opens before you: rich and undulating lands sprinkled with villas, and bounded on one hand by wooded heights and on the other by the grey city, its tin roofs and spires then blazing in the setting sun . . .
>
> Along the road, French faces, with all the harshness of feature and good humour of expression peculiar to the national physiognomy, looked and gossiped from door and window, orchard and meadow, a passing salutation easily winning a smile and courteous obeisance.

Catherine Parr Traill, a resilient emigrant, was less impressed:

> I was greatly disappointed in my first acquaintance with the interior of Montreal; a place of which travellers had said so much . . .
>
> The river-side portion of the town is entirely mercantile. Its narrow, dirty streets and dark houses, with heavy iron shutters, have a disagreeable appearance, which cannot but make an unfavourable impression on the mind of a British traveller. The other portion of the town, however, is of a different character, and the houses are interspersed with gardens and pleasant walks, which looked very agreeable from the windows of the ballroom of the Nelson Hotel.

Anthony Trollope, for once, had no opinion at all:

> Montreal is an exceedingly good commercial town, and business there is brisk. It has now 85,000 inhabitants. Having said that of it, I do not know what more there is left to say.

British visitors found it something of a novelty to come across French culture in North America: 'Montreal is even more *Frenchy* than Quebec,' wrote Captain Horton Rhys, 'and a stranger finds it hard to imagine himself under the sovereignty of H.G.M. the Queen.' But further west, in English-speaking Canada, it was the Englishness which was surprising. Unlike the United States, parts of Canada were distinctly British, as Rhys noted in the town of Hamilton at the western end of Lake Ontario:

> Hamilton is curiously inhabited. There are more Englishmen there without any apparent occupation, and living upon apparently nothing, than in any town in Canada. There are lots of billiard tables, and they (the inhabitants) play;– there is a cricket ground – but I never saw any of *them* there, except in the capacity of lookers on. They seem to be an exiled lot, always looking out for, and expecting something that never turns up. They are constantly in the various stores – i.e. shops – which here are good, without display, but never seem to purchase anything; and, in short, I never could make head or tail of them.

Even the names in this part of Canada were curiously British, London, Ontario, being a small town, complete with its own River Thames. To British visitors, these innocent signs of historical connections with 'the Old Country' amounted to nothing less than cheek, as George Borrett commented, patronizingly:

> If the Canadian Londoners fondly imagine that their little village is worthy to bear the name of its prototype, by all means let them enjoy the innocent delusion. It pleases them, and it does not hurt us.

Western Ontario was often seen by visitors on their way to the continent's major tourist attraction, Niagara Falls, whose description was a required part of any proper account of North America. Amelia Murray, and others, believed that it was 'certainly worth crossing the Atlantic for Niagara alone'.

Anthony Trollope proclaimed Niagara Falls the most impressive sight he had ever seen (including 'all buildings, pictures, statues, and wonders of art made by men's hands, and also the beauties of nature prepared by the Creator for the delight of his creatures'). The most frequent traveller's remark about the Falls was that they were indescribable:

I saw Niagara – Oh God! who can describe that sight!!!
FANNY KEMBLE

I cannot describe them. *most grand! most glorious! IS ALL I CAN SAY.*
THOMAS HAMILTON

Charles Mackay explained the problem:

Any enthusiastic traveller, deeply impressed with the grace, the loveliness, and the sublimity of such a scene, will speedily reach the limits of his vocabulary . . . There are no more adjectives which he can use; but he feels that there is an infinitude of uninvented words in the depths of his consciousness which, if he could but drag them into being, would serve to explain to others how keenly the spiritual beauty of Nature had wrought itself into the spiritual nature of man.

Such apologies were the usual introduction to an elaborate description. Niagara already offered its visitors as much as it does today: it was possible to see the Falls from both the American and Canadian sides, to take a boat trip on the river below, wearing oilskins, and to walk along a ledge of rock behind the cataract.

The fame of Niagara led to prospective visitors arriving in a state of keen anticipation. Basil Hall described his feelings immediately before first seeing the Falls, with an impressive piece of name-dropping:

I remember myself experiencing something akin to it at St Helena, when waiting in Napolean's outer room, under the consciousness that the tread which I heard was from the foot of the man who, a short while before, had roved at will over so great a portion of the world; but whose range was now confined to a few chambers – and that I was separated from this astonishing person, only by a door, which was just about to open. So it was with Niagara. I knew that at the next turn of the road, I should behold the most splendid sight on earth.

'You feel a thrilling, triumphant joy, while contemplating this master-piece of nature – this sublime idea of the Eternal – this wonderful symbol of the power and strength of the divine Architect of the universe.'
SUSANNA MOODIE

Inevitably some visitors were disappointed, and felt guilty and inadequate about their feelings. Anna Brownell Jameson, finding herself unimpressed, indulged in an passion of self-criticism: 'I am an ass's head, a clod, a wooden spoon, a petrifaction.' How many others were too shy to reveal that they had expected more? Many, thought Oscar Wilde:

I was disappointed with Niagara – most people must be disappointed with Niagara. Every American bride is taken there, and the sight of the stupendous waterfall must be one of the earliest, if not the keenest disappointments in American married life.

But for the majority of writers, the Falls were a festival of superlatives:

Never did nature throw together so fantastically so much beauty with such terrific grandeur . . . In the centre of the fall, where the water is heaviest, it takes the leap in an unbroken mass of the deepest green, and in many places reaches the bottom in crystal columns of the same hue, till they meet the snow-white foam that heaves and rolls convulsedly in the enormous basin. But for the deafening roar, the darkness, and the stormy whirlwind in which we stood, I could have fancied these massy volumes the walls of some fairy palace – living emeralds chased in silver.

FRANCES WRIGHT

To say that I was not disappointed is but a weak expression to convey the surprise and astonishment which this long dreamed of scene produced. It has to me something beyond its vastness; there is a shadowy mystery hangs about it which neither the eye nor even the imagination can penetrate; but I dare not dwell on this, it is a dangerous subject, and any attempt to describe the sensations produced must lead direct to nonsense.

FANNY TROLLOPE

Upon my honour, when I found myself crawling along a slimy ledge, with nothing to hold on by but my eyelids, with a few feet of a Mammoth cauldron of mad, ginger-beer-like, unmanufactured-meerschaum-looking liquid, and a solid green wall of ten thousand tons of glancing, sparkling, dazzling water, falling within a few inches of my nose, my own absurd smallness became momentarily so uncomfortably apparent, that I thereupon set such an inconceivable amount of value on what there was of me, my whole, sole, and only thought was, 'If ever I get safely out of this, you'll never catch me in it again!' And having penetrated as far as the guide, in dumb show, informed me, anybody goes, I slipped, sidled, and finally sloped back to my party.

CAPTAIN HORTON RHYS

All this sensory excitement was followed by a state of reflective composure, through which a burst of nervous energy could suddenly break. For the usually rational Captain Marryat, this was, apparently, a moment of great personal danger:

For about half an hour more I continued to watch the rolling waters, and then I felt a slight dizziness and a creeping sensation come over me – that sensation arising from strong excitement, and the same, probably, that occasions the bird to fall into the jaws of the snake. This is a feeling which, if too long indulged in, becomes irresistible, and occasions a craving desire to leap into the flood of rushing waters. It increased upon me every minute; and, retreating from the brink, I turned my eyes to the surrounding foliage until the effect of the excitement had passed away.

The Falls also had a spiritual element: like a range of mountains, or a stormy ocean, they presented the sensitive tourist with a humbling insight into humanity's place in the world, and could produce a transcendental experience, as Anthony Trollope explained:

'We emerged in safety, but drenched to the skin, notwithstanding our india-rubber preservatives.'
CLARA BROMLEY

To realize Niagara you must sit there till you see nothing else than that which you have come to see. You will hear nothing else, and think of nothing else. At length you will be at one with the tumbling river before you. You will find yourself among the waters as though you belonged to them. The cool liquid green will run through your veins, and the voice of the cataract will be the expression of your own heart. You will fall as the bright waters fall, rushing down into your new world with no hesitation and with no dismay; and you will rise again as the spray rises, bright beautiful, and pure. Then you will flow away in your course to the uncompassed, distant, and eternal ocean.

As a Methodist minister, James Dixon enjoyed an almost religious insight at the Falls:

I sat silent and motionless a long time, looking with a sort of vacant astonishment at the whole scene. The thoughts, 'It is grand! it is sublime! it is awful!' crossed my mind, but nothing definite had fixed itself there; all remained in the same confusion, chaos, stupefaction. At length, as if awaking from a dream, I exclaimed, 'How beautiful!' And then, in a moment, a thrill ran through my soul like an electric shock, which at once scattered the mists; and I exclaimed, loud enough to have been heard, 'Ah yes, that is it, that is it, – it belongs to the beautiful.' This was a new idea, a revelation, and transformed the whole scene in an instant into perfect unity and glory.

Even Dickens found the experience brought him into contact with God:

When I felt how near to my Creator I was standing, the first effect, and the enduring one – instant and lasting – of the tremendous spectacle, was Peace. Peace of Mind, Tranquillity, Calm recollections of the Dead, Great Thoughts of Eternal Rest and Happiness: nothing of Gloom or Terror. Niagara was at once stamped upon my heart, an Image of Beauty; to remain there, changeless and indelible, until its pulses cease to beat, for ever.

Basil Hall doesn't reveal whether Napoleon lived up to his anticipation of their meeting; but the Falls certainly exceeded his expectations. Hall revisited them several times, concluding with an extended meditation in front of the cataract for three hours, a time he later claimed had been 'the most interesting of my whole life':

I was almost overwhelmed – if that be the proper word to use - with the grandeur of this extraordinary spectacle. I felt, as it were, staggered and confused, and at times experienced a sensation bordering on alarm . . . The influence of one overpowering but indefinite sensation at times absorbed the active operation of the senses, and produced a kind of dizzy reverie, more or less akin to sleep, or rather to the intoxication described by opium eaters, during which a thousand visions arose connected with the general sentiment of sublimity. And it may help to give some idea of the extravagent length to which the over-indulged fancy can carry the dreamer on such occasions, to mention that once, for some seconds, I caught myself thinking that I had fairly left this lower world for the upper sky, – that I was traversing the Heavens in company with Sir Isaac Newton, – and that the Sage was just going to tell me about the distance of the fixed stars.

Her feet firmly on the ground, Mrs Jameson remained unimpressed, but deeply disturbed:

I have beheld them, and shall I whisper it to you! – but, O tell it not among the Philistines – I wish I had not! I wish they were still a thing unbeheld – a thing to be imagined, hoped, and anticipated – something to live for: – the reality has displaced from my mind an illusion far more magnificent than itself – I have no words for my utter disappointment: yet I have not the presumption to suppose that all I have heard and read of Niagara is false or exaggerated – that every expression of astonishment, enthusiasm, rapture, is affectation or hyperbole. No! it must be my own fault.

The Falls were an impressive exhibition of the natural world, but they occupied only a few acres. Even more impressive, to those willing to risk the unpredictable, was the experience of the vastness of the continent, stretching west further than a mind familiar with the distances of Britain could even imagine.

CHAPTER THIRTEEN

A Gazetteer of Western Development

With the odd exception such as Kipling, who travelled from California to the Atlantic on his way to England from his native India, British visitors experienced North America from east to west. As the century progressed, it became possible to journey further and further into the continent. The American and Canadian populations were moving west, and the more adventurous visitors followed.

There was no dividing line between settled, civilized eastern cities, and frenzied, half-built western ones; there was a spectrum of change from east to west, with the drift of population following the improvement of roads, the digging of canals and the laying of railway track, as Charles Mackay explained in 1858:

> In America the 'West' is very difficult to fix. Ask the people of Cincinnati, and they will tell you it is at St. Louis. At St. Louis it is at Utah, the paradise of the Mormons. At Utah the West is in Oregon; and at Oregon it is in California or Vancouver's Island, and the shores of the Pacific Ocean.

In the eyes of visitors, neither the settled, nor the rapidly developing city held the monopoly of virtue. Where one writer saw a depressing mess of mud, hacked timber and crowds of money-minded entrepreneurs, another would see the expressions of courage and optimism, and marvel at the energy with which 'improvements' were being made.

Time itself transformed the fortunes of a developing city: the Toronto of 1836, as seen by Anna Brownell Jameson, had little to offer a visitor in search of entertainment. She described it viciously:

> A little ill-built town on low land, at the bottom of a frozen bay, with one very ugly church, without tower or steeple; some government offices, built of staring red brick, in the most tasteless, vulgar style imaginable; three feet of snow all around; and the gray, sullen,

wintry lake, and the dark gloom of the pine forest bounding the prospect; such seems Toronto to me now. I did not expect much; but for this I was not prepared . . . Toronto is like a fourth- or fifth-rate provincial town with the pretensions of a capital city. We have here a petty oligarchy, a self-constituted aristocracy, based upon nothing real, nor even upon anything imaginary . . . We have here conventionalism in its most oppressive and ridiculous forms.

It was only six years later, when the city cannot have been much different, that Charles Dickens found Toronto 'full of life and motion, bustle, business, and improvement. The streets are well-paved, and lighted with gas; the houses are large and good; the shops excellent.' And Susanna Moodie, a decade after that, was positively inspired by its atmosphere:

There is a fresh, growing, healthy vitality about this place, that cannot fail to impress a stranger very forcibly the first time he enters it. He feels instinctively that he sees before him the strong throbbing heart of this gigantic young country, and that every powerful vibration from this ever increasing centre of wealth and civilisation, infuses life and vigour through the whole length and breadth of the province.

A city even more famous for the vigour of its growth was Chicago. It was incorporated in 1837, with a population of 4,000. Anthony Trollope visited in 1861, and was amazed at what he found:

Chicago is in many respects the most remarkable city among all the remarkable cities of the Union. Its growth has been the fastest and its success the most assured. Twenty-five years ago there was no Chicago, and now it contains 120,000 inhabitants . . .
  In Chicago there are great streets, and rows of houses fit to be the residences of a new Corn Exchange nobility. They look out on the wide lake which is now the highway for breadstuffs, and the merchant, as he shaves at his window, sees his rapid ventures as they pass away, one after the other, towards the East.

Ten years after Trollope's visit, most of the city was destroyed in a great fire, which left 90,000 people homeless. There was an international appeal for help; one of those who responded, in Scotland, was the young Robert Louis Stevenson. Eight years later, in 1879, he was able to inspect the city, which had, by then, become considerably more prosperous than its patron:

Chicago seemed a great and gloomy city. I remember having subscribed, let us say sixpence, towards its restoration at the period of the fire; and now when I beheld street after street of comfortable burghers, I thought it would be a graceful act for the corporation to refund that sixpence, or, at least to entertain me to a cheerful dinner. But there was no word of restitution. I was the city's benefactor, yet I was received in a third-class waiting-room, and the best dinner I could get was a dish of ham and eggs at my own expense.

William Fraser Rae described Chicago as 'the paradise of the modern man of business'; indeed, its growth to a population of over a million by the turn of the century proved him right. Rae found the climate heady: 'compared with the bustle of Chicago, the bustle of New York seems stagnation . . . none but the idle starve: none but the stupid die poor.'

Chicago was only one of many American cities growing rapidly, some of which had earlier origins. During the 1860s Chicago was beginning to rival Cincinnati in an important industry, the slaughtering of pigs. Cincinnati was the final destination of almost half a million pigs a year, and their presence had been a feature of visitors' accounts since Mrs Trollope described the scene in 1828:

It hardly seems fair to quarrel with a place because its staple commodity is not pretty, but I am sure I should have liked Cincinnati much better if the people had not dealt so very largely in hogs. The immense quantity of business done in this line would hardly be believed by those who had not witnessed it. I never saw a newspaper without remarking such advertisements as the following:

'Wanted, immediately, 4,000 fat hogs.'
'For sale, 2,000 barrels of prime pork.'

But the annoyance came nearer than this: if I determined upon a walk up Main-street, then chances were five hundred to one against my reaching the shady side without brushing by a snout fresh dripping from the kennel; when we had screwed our courage to the enterprise of mounting a certain noble-looking sugar-loaf hill, that promised pure air and a fine view, we found the brook we had to cross, at its foot, red with the stream from a pig slaughter house; while our noses, instead of meeting 'the thyme that loves that green hill's breast', were greeted by odours that I will not describe, and which I heartily hope my readers cannot imagine.

Charles Weld picked up the story during his *Vacation Tour* of 1855:

The picture given by Mrs Trollope of the condition of the streets at the period of her residence in Cincinnati in 1828 holds good now . . . It must not be supposed, however, that the Cincinnati pigs are allowed to lead a long life of vagabondism. When their numbers increase by births and immigration to about six thousand, they are collected and sold by

'Chicago is a sort of monster-shop, full of bustle and bores.'

OSCAR WILDE

auction for the benefit of the city. Prior to this event, any person may capture a pig if he can, – for the Cincinnati pigs have a wonderful facility of locomotion, – and kill it *pro bono familias*: hear this, ye natives of the Emerald Isle, whose height of ambition and fortune is the possession of one porker.

Emerging American cities, growing on the strength of their industries, could still offer the visitor more traditional civic attractions. Charles Dickens' description of Cincinnati ignored its noisy, macabre industry altogether: 'Cincinnati is a beautiful city; cheerful, thriving and animated. I have not often seen a place that commends itself so favourably and pleasantly to a stranger at first glance.' And cities which have since acquired their character through heavy industry began more gently. Anna Brownell Jameson visited Detroit, Michigan, in 1838:

Of all the places I have yet seen in these far western regions, Detroit is the most interesting. It is, moreover, a most ancient and venerable place, dating back to the dark immemorial ages, *i.e.* almost a century and a quarter ago!
 . . . The crowd of emigrants constantly pouring through this little city on their way to the back settlements of the west, and the number of steamers, brigs, and a schooners always passing up and down the lakes, occasion a perpetual bustle, variety and animation on the shore and in the streets.

Captain Marryat found that social life in Detroit was pursued fastidiously, despite the obstacles:

In winter, in rainy weather you are up to your knees in mud; in summer, invisible from dust; indeed, until recently there was not a practicable road for thirty miles round Detroit. The muddy and impassable state of the streets has given rise to a very curious system of making morning or evening calls. A small one-horse cart is backed against the door of a house; the ladies dressed get into it, and seat themselves upon a buffalo-skin at the bottom of it; they are carried to the residence of the party upon whom they wish to call; the cart is backed in again, and they are landed dry and clean.

Whether such complications were seen as amusing or irritating depended on the traveller, or perhaps on how the traveller was feeling that day. Anthony Trollope was not impressed with Detroit:

It is not so pleasant as Milwaukee, nor so picturesque as St. Paul, nor so grand as Chicago, nor so civilised as Cleveland, nor so busy as Buffalo. Indeed, Detroit is neither pleasant nor picturesque at all. I will not say that it is uncivilised, but it has a harsh, crude unprepossessing appearance . . . I do not, however, think it well to recommend any Englishman to make a special visit to Detroit.

Round the other side of Lake Erie in Cleveland, Ohio, Trollope was again less than generous:

These houses in Cleveland were very good, – as indeed they are in most Northern towns; but some of them have been erected with an amount of bad taste that is almost incredible. It is not uncommon to see in front of a square brick house a wooden quasi-Greek portico, with a pediment and Ionic columns, equally high with the house itself.

George Borrett, who travelled at almost the same time as Trollope, came to exactly the opposite view of Cleveland:

It is a very pretty place, much like Buffalo, though of smaller dimensions; but more tastefully laid out, especially in the suburbs, where the merchants' houses are really beautiful. Certainly these Americans have wonderful taste.

Even Trollope was not uniformly rude about these northern cities. He sometimes developed a quite unpredictable liking, as for Milwaukee, Wisconsin:

How many of my readers can boast that they know anything of Milwaukee, or even have heard of it? To me its name was unknown until I saw it on huge railway placards stuck up in the smoking-rooms and lounging halls of all American hotels. It is the big town of Wisconsin, whereas Madison is the capital. It stands immediately on the western shore of Lake Michigan, and is very pleasant. Why it should be so, and why Detroit should be the contrary, I can hardly tell; only I think that the same verdict would be given by any English tourist.

Here the tables were turned, and it was Borrett whose account, albeit somewhat more benevolent than some of Trollope's, is that of a man who has seen too much too quickly:

There is nothing in Milwaukee but what may be found in every other American city that I have seen, and I believe in all that I have not seen. Long straight handsome streets, wide boulevards, enormous hotels, colossal warehouses, gigantic stores, spacious wharves, and cyclopean 'elevators'; a large imposing post office, three or four passable churches, advertisements upon any vacant surface, a railway station in the middle of the high street, tracks for street cars everywhere, good paving nowhere; crowds in the stores, at the entrance to the hotels, in the street cars, and round the offices of the local journals; buggies rushing in all directions, always apparently late for a train, like the butchers' carts in London; abundance of colour, plenty of noise, tobacco-smoke, heat, and dust.

As Borrett said, there was much in common between different cities, most of them success stories of rapid development. Growth was fast enough to be obvious to visitors. Captain Marryat visited Buffalo in 1838:

Buffalo is one of the wonders of America. It is hardly to be credited that such a beautiful city could have risen up in the wilderness in so short a period . . . The main street is wider and the stores handsomer than the majority of those in New York. It has five or six very fine churches, a handsome theatre, town hall and market, and three or four hotels, one of which is superior to most others in America . . . It is almost incomprehensible that all this should have been accomplished since the year 1814.

Further west, the same story could be told, beginning later than in the east. Over a thousand miles west and north of Buffalo, the Canadian city of Winnipeg, Manitoba, was booming in the late 1880s. By then, visitors like Edward Roper could arrive by train. Roper found what he considered a surprisingly cosmopolitan city:

I found a very large proportion of good, kind people there, people who have lived in, or who have visited other lands, and who know what's what. There were others we met, good, kind folks too, who yet were quite indignant, or appeared to be so, if we did not declare right off that this ten-year-old city was far ahead of any other place we have ever seen in the New World or the Old.

Rudyard Kipling was struck by the way cities like Winnipeg were pushing development further and further west, their new asphalt streets and concrete sidewalks holding back the prairie mud: 'where the daring road ended, there lay unsubdued, level with the pale asphalt, the tenacious prairie, over which civilisation found her hub-deep way to the West. And with asphalt and concrete they fight the prairie back every building season.' •

In some places, the wave of speculators seemed to run far ahead of the advancing population. Anthony Trollope arrived in St Paul, Minnesota, and wondered whether it would ever bustle and grow rich like the other places he had seen:

Look at the map, and see where St. Paul is. Its distance from all known civilisation, – all civilisation that has succeeded in obtaining acquaintance with the world at large, is very great. Even American travellers do not go up there in great numbers, excepting those who intend to settle there . . . Nevertheless an hotel has been built there capable of holding three hundred guests, and other hotels exist in the neighbourhood, one of which is even larger than that at St. Paul. Who can come to them, and create even a hope that such an enterprise may be remunerative?

Inevitably, there were businesses that failed, but if they had assets, like a hotel, the assets were taken over and made profitable by somebody else. It was hard for a pioneer businessman or farmer to overestimate the speed of development. The arrival of the railway was a catalyst like no other; a city could leap into existence in a matter of days, as W. Henry Barneby witnessed in Calgary, Alberta, in 1883:

Calgary is quite in its infancy. There has been a Hudson's Bay Company's Fort here for some years, and also a police barracks, but no other inhabited place. On the approach of the railway, however, a sudden spurt has taken place, as is shown by the great influx of visitors within the last ten to fourteen days. Fifty to sixty tents and framed houses have already sprung up. There are hotels, stores, & c., and more people are on the road; so the cry is certainly 'Still they come.'

We went to the 'Royal Hotel,' a tent about thirty feet long by eighteen feet broad, and decided to take up our quarters there for the night.

A few years later, Edward Roper gave a typical account of the developing city: he found Calgary 'very much like most places of the kind we had yet seen – new, rough, unhappy-looking, but decidedly prosperous'. And this was the pattern until the trail and track ended at the Pacific. In the north, the ocean bordered the huge, wooded colony of British Columbia. Rudyard Kipling was almost tempted to settle there:

British Columbia appears to be the richest and the loveliest section of the Continent . . . Were I an intending immigrant I would risk a good deal of discomfort to get on to the land in British Columbia; and were I rich, with no attachments outside England, I would swiftly buy me a farm or a house in that country for the mere joy of it.

Before the development of Vancouver, the main town in the region was Victoria, on Vancouver Island. Kipling described its situation with a knowledgeable eye:

To realize Victoria you must take all that the eye admires most in Bournemouth, Torquay, the Isle of Wight, the Happy Valley at Hong Kong, the Doon, Sorrento, and Camps Bay; add reminiscences of the Thousand Islands, and arrange the whole round the Bay of Naples, with some Himalayas for the background.

R. Byron Johnson, in 1862, observed that, to its inhabitants, the attractions of Victoria were more immediate:

The average Victorian's sense of bliss apparently consists of the largest possible number of drinks in the shortest possible time, varied with cigars and billiards *ad lib*. The number of billiard-tables is simply astonishing to English eyes: there are at least eighty to a town of five or six thousand inhabitants, and they seem to be kept well going day and night.

Johnson was witnessing the height of the local goldrush. Twenty years later, in 1883, when W. Henry Barneby visited, he was able to report that 'although Victoria is a very nice place, it is rather a sleepy one'.

The fact that the emerging city of Vancouver was not on Vancouver Island was the source of much confusion: Mrs E.H.Carbutt, on tour in 1888, suggested it would have been more convenient if 'this little village' had kept its former name, Fort Moody. In the same year, Edward Roper recorded optimistically:

The people of Vancouver City have much to be proud of, and are justified in boasting. Its natural advantages are very great; no finer site could have been chosen for a commercial town . . . There is ample room for the cultivation of everything that can be needed for ages to come. The climate is everything that is desirable. What more can be required to insure the success and unbounded prosperity of this city? To crown all, the British flag floats over the country.

Further south, in the United States, San Francisco, whose origins were earlier, displayed all the vigour of American development. As in New York, British visitors were impressed with their first sight of the city. In 1879 Robert Louis Stevenson had been travelling by train across the continent:

The day was breaking as we crossed the ferry; the fog was rising over the citied hills of San Francisco; the bay was perfect – not a ripple, scarce a stain, upon its blue expanse; everything was waiting, breathless, for the sun. A spot of cloudy gold lit first upon the head of Tamalpais . . . and the city of San Francisco, and the bay of gold and corn, were lit from end to end with summer daylight.

For William Fraser Rae, San Francisco appeared to best advantage from a distance:

Built on a hill slope, up which many streets run to the top, and illuminated as these streets were with innumerable gas lamps, the effect was that of a huge dome ablaze with lamps

'Truly the energy exhibited in building (San Francisco), and overcoming the natural disadvantages of its position, was, and still is, immense.'

R. BYRON JOHNSON

arranged in lines and circles. Those who have stood in Princes Street at night, and gazed upon the Old Town and Castle of Edinburgh, can form a very correct notion of the fairy-like spectacle.

If this spectacle be poetry the landing is prose. The din and bustle soon recall the errant mind from aerial flights of fancy to the harsh realities of terrestrial life. A Babel of tongues rises from the crowded landing-stage as soon as the steamer has been moored. Hardly has the passenger set foot on shore than he becomes the prey of men intent upon earning a gratuity by doing, or professing to render, him a service.

R. Byron Johnson, on his way north to British Columbia, confirmed this account, down to the same biblical metaphor:

The bustle and noise were terrific. The row caused by the numberless omnibuses, drays, and street cars, running over the plank roads, was deafening; and this was supplemented by the hoarse hooting of the various steamboats whistles, the incessant buzz of the hotel touter, the cracking of whips, and curses at the unwilling quadrupeds; forming altogether a Babel which it is hardly possible to realise without actual experience.

Rudyard Kipling was enchanted with the city, even though he found it overwhelming:

San Francisco is a mad city – inhabited for the most part by perfectly insane people whose women are of a remarkable beauty . . . The cable cars have for all practical purposes made San Francisco a dead level. They take no account of rise or fall, but slide equally on their appointed courses from one end to the other of a six-mile street. They turn corners almost at right angles; cross other lines, and, for aught I know, may run up the sides of houses. There is no visible agency of their flight; but once in a while you shall pass a five-storied building, humming with machinery that winds up an everlasting wire-cable, and the initiated will tell you that here is the mechanism. I gave up asking questions. If it pleases Providence to make a car run up and down a slit in the ground for many miles, and if for twopence-halfpenny I can ride in that car, why shall I seek the reasons of the miracle?

On the east coast, the British could compare and contrast what they saw with what they knew at home: men in Congress were scruffier than Members of Parliament, the New York shops sold more French furniture than those in London, and the hotels were larger. Here in the west (or what Johnson, in the title of his book of travels, called *Very Far West Indeed*), life was different enough to be taken on its own terms. Everyone was part of the adventure: the inhabitants may only have arrived in the city a day or two before the tourists, and all were expected to make the best of what they found. This was California, or, as Kipling called it, Fairyland, 'where cherries were as big as plums, plums as big as apples, and strawberries of no account; where the procession of fruits of the season was like a pageant in a Drury Lane pantomime and where the dry air was wine'. Isabella Bird picked up the theme:

California is a 'land flowing with milk and honey'. The barns are bursting with fulness. In the dusty orchards the apple and pear branches are supported, that they may not break down under the weight of fruit; melons, tomatoes, and squashes of gigantic size lie almost unheeded on the ground; fat cattle, gorged almost to repletion, shade themselves under the oaks; superb 'red' horses shine, not with grooming, but with condition; and thriving farms everywhere show on what a solid basis the prosperity of the 'Golden State' is founded.

Along with the Fairyland fruit, there was a second, equally Californian tradition: R. Byron Johnson described the violence of the streets:

> It is not to be wondered at that, in its early days, a place offering such wondrous attractions to all classes as California did, should have been the home of a greater number of thorough-paced scoundrels than the collected vice of the rest of the world could well have produced. Mexican horse thieves and bandits, runaway Australian convicts, gamblers from all the cities of the Union, border ruffians from the Western States, and rogues of different degrees from all parts, were abundant; the revolver and the bowie-knife were the aggressors and the arbiters, and justice was a farce.

To most British visitors, the natural beauties of California more than compensated for a little lawlessness. Oscar Wilde wrote of California's 'eternal summer' with 'groves of orange trees in fruit and flower, green fields, and purple hills, a very Italy without art'. And Charles Kingsley reported that 'all is more beautiful and wonderful than I expected, and California the finest country in the world – and oh! the flowers'.

Isabella Bird described a Californian sight which has since thrilled generations of tourists:

> I have found a dream of beauty at which one might look all one's life and sigh . . . A strictly North American beauty – snow-splotched mountains, huge pines, red-woods, sugar pines, silver spruce; a crystalline atmosphere, waves of the richest colour; and a pine-hung lake which mirrors all beauty on its surface. Lake Tahoe is before me, a sheet of water twenty-two miles long by ten broad, and in some places 1700 feet deep.

For all the advantages of their state, Californians suffered their own particular form of a general national sensitivity to British opinion, according to William Fraser Rae:

> Among the earliest questions put by an American lady or gentleman to a traveller from England who lands at Boston, New York, or Baltimore this one is certain to be included: – 'How do you like America?' If, however, the traveller should first tread the sacred soil of the Union when stepping ashore at San Francisco, he will as certainly be asked: – 'What do you think of California?' In the former case, the reply is expected that America is a great country; in the latter, that California is a paradise.

California had been colonized by the Spanish, but became part of Mexico when Mexico won independence from Spain in 1821. In the 1840s the United States won a war against Mexico, and by 1850, California had joined the Union. But places like Monterey, further down the coast from San Francisco, still had a history and culture quite different from that of the rest of the United States. Robert Louis Stevenson went to Monterey, and loved its artistic foreign atmosphere, so different from the hard commercialism of the rest of English-speaking America:

> The Mexicans, you may say, are all poor and landless, like their former capital; and yet both it and they hold themselves apart and preserve their ancient customs and something of their ancient air . . . Night after night serenaders would be going about the street, sometimes in a company and with several instruments and voices together, sometimes severally, each guitar before a different window. It was a strange thing to lie awake in nineteenth-century America, and hear the guitar accompany, and one of these old, heart-breaking Spanish love songs mount into the night air.

Los Angeles was rarely visited by tourists, being a small, unremarkable town. W. Henry Barneby reported in 1883 that: 'contrary to our expectations, Los Angeles is not at all a pretty place. It seemed markedly Spanish in its aspect and manners.' Nevertheless, Barneby and his party, accompanied by the Mayor of Los Angeles, were 'regaled with cake and mint julep' by the owner of a local vineyard, and found a hotel with a view of the Pacific, where Barneby 'with a cigar and an arm-chair, and my feet well out of my bed-room window, succeeded in making myself very comfortable for a bit'. He ordered ten gallons of Californian port and ten gallons of wine to be sent back to his home in Herefordshire to await his return.

Mrs E.H.Carbutt, in 1888, reported:

> We spent a day exploring Los Angeles, which appeared to be very prosperous and growing rapidly. The residential quarters are exceedingly pretty, each house having a garden planted with orange-trees, aloes, & c., and coming down to the edge of the road . . . We noticed that Los Angeles ladies are very pretty.

For all this, Mrs Carbutt was not optimistic about the prospects for southern California as a tourist area. She noted that 'immense hotels have been built everywhere' to attract winter visitors in search of the sun; but they were empty, because 'there are very few attractions in California. There are no roads for driving or preparations of any kind for tourists.'

As far south as one could travel down the west coast of the United States was San Diego. Again, reports from this period are rare, but one, from William Shaw in 1849, leaves the long trek across the continent on a festive note, suggesting that the accidents of a journey, and the people met by chance are the real key to the contentment of a traveller:

> The principal houses of Diego surround a spacious square, in the centre of which, flanked by two pieces of heavy artillery, stands a lofty flag-staff, from which floats the American

banner; an additional star on which, reminds the haughty Spaniards of their subjugation . . . Availing myself of the hospitable repute of the residents, I entered boldly several houses. In one of them, after passing through several apartments, I espied its inmates in what I imagine was the kitchen: the lady of the house, a stout, matronly dame, was scolding in shrill tones some black domestics who were pounding maize, while around her were grouped three beautiful blushing damsels. The old lady did not seem in the least disconcerted at my intrusion; saying 'Buenos dias, Señor,' she, after a short conference, led the way to an elegant apartment, followed by her daughters. The latter understood a little English, and we soon became acquainted; during my residence at Diego I visited the family constantly, and the senora placed much confidence in me. The daughters had none of the prudery habitual to European girls; and we passed many pleasant hours smoking cigarettes together in the observatory at the top of the house.

CHAPTER FOURTEEN

WRITING AND OTHER BUSINESS

*I am overworked, overdined, oversupped, overvisited – three days ago I fell
ill and have passed two since in great pain and comfort in my bedroom*

WILLIAM MAKEPEACE THACKERAY

Thackeray's letters home during his North American lecture tours in the 1850s reveal an impatience with his laborious travels. The south was especially hot and uncomfortable. If writing was one per cent inspiration and ninety-nine per cent perspiration, the American lecture circuit was the same. Thackeray vented his irritation to his British correspondents. Yet, beneath the frustration was a smug satisfaction: 'as far as the money goes, I am doing great things here & the dollars are rolling in.'

Oscar Wilde, on tour in 1882, was more enthusiastic about the whirl of crowds and the travelling, and wrote home, gloating, that his audience in New York had been 'larger and more wonderful than Dickens ever had'. Wilde was the complete celebrity, trailed by reporters hoping to catch a witty remark, and attended by several secretaries: 'one writes my autographs all day for my admirers, the other receives the flowers that are left really every ten minutes. A third whose hair resembles mine is obliged to send off locks of his own hair to the myriad maidens of the city, and so is rapidly becoming bald.' For all the fun, Wilde was as interested in Thackeray in his income; he described the tour as 'dreadfully hard work', but hoped to make enough money from it to pay for 'an autumn at Venice, a winter at Rome, and a spring at Athens'. In fact, he spent the proceeds on three months in Paris.

Every writer had different, usually mixed, motives for the journey to North America, of which the written account itself was anything from a central reason, to an unplanned by-product. Those travelling with no particular intention of publishing an account may have failed to record each telling detail as it happened, but the diligent note-taker suffered from a different kind of limitation, that of being warily observed by those who knew they were themselves being watched. In company, Captain Marryat, a professional writer, found that: 'everyone appeared afraid to speak; and when anything ludicrous occurred, the cry would be –

"Oh, now, Captain Marryat, don't put that in your book."' Marryat thought the Americans deliberately tried to mislead anyone who was planning to write about their country. After three weeks he decided to refuse all invitations to private homes. With this self-imposed restriction, he still believed he could reveal something about their country which Americans had not been able to spot for themselves: 'the remarks of a traveller in any country not his own, let his work be ever so trifling or badly written, will point out some peculiarity which will have escaped the notice of those who were born and reside in that country.'

British writers generally had confidence that a fresh eye would reveal a kind of truth to which the natives were blind. Basil Hall especially valued first impressions, and tried to convey his heightened perception on arriving in a country. Gliding up the Hudson in a steamer, he wondered about the reality of the scene; had it come into existence a moment earlier, for his benefit?

> In many other parts of the world I have felt something of the same kind; and have frequently caught myself, in distant countries, looking with surprise at the people bustling about and attending to their ordinary affairs, with what seemed a stupid unconsciousness of the curiosity of appearances to me so new and so wondrous strange. Of course, in the next instant, such fantastic delusions would flit off, and give place to more substantial impressions . . . The pleasures of travelling, taken in this spirit, will sometimes far exceed the anticipation; and those brilliant pictures drawn by early enthusiasm or even by matured curiosity, of the wonders of the world, are often feeble in their colouring, compared to that of the actual original viewed on the spot.

If the writer could only capture the vivid, unvarnished scene, so the theory went, then neither reader nor subject could complain. Thomas Hamilton unashamedly recorded subjective impressions, and admitted that his sources of information were fallible:

> The range of a traveller's observations must generally be limited to those peculiarities which float, as it were, on the surface of society. Of the 'sunken treasures' beneath, he cannot speak.

While disclaimers like these were often included in the introduction to a volume of travels, it was easy for the reader, and, it seems, the writer, to forget them a few hundred pages later. By then, the writer's grand theories and sometimes savage criticisms seemed much more than mere innocent observations. Frances Wright was wary of subjectivity, and cautioned against generalizations drawn from notes written at the end of a weary day:

'It is often useful in travelling, to record at the instant those trivial but peculiar circumstances, which first strike the eye of a stranger, since, in a short time, they become so familiar as entirely to escape attention.'

BASIL HALL

A traveller is, of all men, most at the mercy of these nameless trifles; it is a pity, however, that nations should be laid at their mercy too, or rather at the mercy of a jaded traveller's distempered mind. Would it not be a good rule that when a tourist sits down with pen and paper before him to pass judgment upon the world around him, he should first ask himself a few questions: 'Am I in good health and good humour? in a comfortable room and an easy chair? at peace with myself and all men about me?' I have a notion that some such short catechism would save volumes of misstated facts and misrepresented characters and keep the peace not only between man and man, but nation and nation.

Thomas Hamilton's account of working one evening on a crowded steamboat is a textbook example of what Wright was worried about:

If I wrote in bad humour there was really some excuse for it. Close to my right were two loud polemics, engaged in fierce disputation on the Tariff bill. On my left was an elderly gentleman, without shoes or slippers, whose cough and expectoration were somewhat less melodious than the music of the spheres. In the berth immediately behind, lay a passenger, whose loud snoring proclaimed him as happy as a complete oblivion of all worldly cares could make him. Right opposite was a gentleman without breeches, who, before jumping into bed, was detailing to a friend the particulars of a lucky hit he had just made in a speculation in train oil. And beside me, at the table, sat a Baptist clergyman, reading, *sotto voce*, a chapter of Ezekiel, and casting, at the conclusion of each verse, a glance of furtive curiosity at my paper.

Was this the evening on which Hamilton recorded his harsh verdict on the town of Hartford, Connecticut?

I wandered about the town, saw the College and the New Exchange Buildings, and a church and a gaol, and a school, and the Charter oak, and peeped into all the shops, and then returned to the inn with the assured conviction that Hartford is one of the stupidest places on the surface of the globe.

The residents of Hartford were among many sections of the North American population to have their noses put out of joint by the jottings of British writers. The often-repeated British charge of American over-sensitivity to criticism could, surely, only account for a fraction of the distress caused. The writers themselves were aware of the reputation of previous accounts, and often tried to distinguish their own project as being more serious, more sensitive, and better informed than those of their predecessors:

By many of the writers on America, the little discrepancies, the mere trifles of custom have been dwelt upon, with a sarcastic, ill-natured severity to give their works that semblance of pith, in which, in reality, they were miserably deficient; and they violated the rights of hospitality that they might increase their interest as authors.

CAPTAIN MARRYAT

In dealing with America, the reader has been long enough amused by different writers, at the expense of his confidence. It is high time that portraiture superceded caricature.

ALEXANDER MACKAY

Similarly, Tyrone Power castigated previous writers for concentrating on 'spitting-boxes, tobacco, two-pronged forks or other conventional *bagatelles*' and James Dixon complained of fashionable English writers expecting America to mimic the styles of the West End: 'what right can the flippant dames, the military beaux, the panderers to frivolity, have to expect a people ready made to their several purposes?' William Fraser Rae found that Americans had become so used to being insulted that 'a notion is prevalent that the majority of English travellers visit America solely in order to accumulate materials wherewith to fill volumes with sneers and abuse.'

According to other travellers, Fanny Trollope's was the single more influential book. Published in 1832, it was one of the earliest, and was widely read on both sides of the Atlantic. In Canada, Susanna Moodie suffered from its unpopularity, but had no reservations about its content:

> I was told by a lady, the very first time I appeared in company, that 'she heard that I wrote books, but she could tell me that they did not want a Mrs Trollope in Canada.'
>
> I had not then read Mrs Trollope's work on America, or I should have comprehended at once the cause of her indignation; for she was just such a person as would have drawn forth the keen satire of that far-seeing observer of the absurdities of our nature, whose witty exposure of American affectation has done more towards producing a reform in that respect, than would have resulted from a thousand grave animadversions soberly written.

Captain Marryat, visiting Cincinnati, where Mrs Trollope lived for most of the time she described in her book, reported that the inhabitants thought she had been 'very severe and very unjust' in her depiction of life in their city. Marryat relayed the explanation of one local as to why Mrs Trollope found their society so lacking in social graces: as an unknown married woman travelling without her husband, Marryat was told, Mrs Trollope was viewed with suspicion by the 'best society'. As a result, she 'did not receive those attentions, the omission of which caused her indignation'. Marryat believed that ten years later she had been forgiven

THE WRITERS

FANNY TROLLOPE (1780–1863) wrote her first book, *Domestic Manners of the Americans* (1832), when she was over fifty, in an attempt to improve the finances of her family. Her husband was an unsuccessful lawyer and farmer, and the couple had six children. Fanny took the three youngest to America with her in 1827, arriving back in England fifteen months later. Her book, with its indignant complaints and entertaining stories, was a huge success, and brought further publishing contracts, for follow-ups about France, Belgium and Austria. The family lived in various European countries as Fanny worked on what became a total of more than forty books, including novels. She had solved the family's financial problems, and built a literary career on her forthright views of America: 'we received, as I have mentioned, much personal kindness,' she wrote, 'but this by no means interfered with the national feeling of, I believe, unconquerable dislike, which evidently lives at the bottom of every truly American heart against the English.'

because 'Americans, although appearances are certainly very much against it, are really, at the bottom, a very good-tempered people'.

Mrs Trollope's reputation was of more than usual interest to her son, the novelist Anthony Trollope, who followed in her footsteps thirty years later to write his own account of North America. In its introduction, he described his mother's book as 'well-known and successful', but explained that his own efforts would be directed towards balancing what had been 'essentially a woman's book'; he believed his mother had described the laughable but temporary effects of establishing the American political system. Trollope worried about his own task, explaining to his readers how his 'light pen' was also in danger of giving offence: 'it is hard to write about any country a book that does not represent the country described in a more or less ridiculous point of view,' he pleaded.

Two volumes later, Trollope concluded with a troubled apology for what he had written, not knowing whether to blame himself or the Americans for the further offence he believed he had given:

> I have ever admired the United States as a nation. I have loved their liberty, their prowess, their intelligence, and their progress. I have sympathized with a people who themselves had no sympathy with passive security and inaction. I have felt confidence in them, and have known, as it were, that their industry must enable them to succeed as a people, while their freedom would insure to them success as a nation. With these convictions I went among them wishing to write of them good words, – words which might be pleasant for them to read, while they might assist perhaps in producing a true impression of them here at home. But among my good words there are so many which are bitter, that I fear I shall have failed in my object as regards them. And it seems to me, as I read once more my own pages, that in saying evil things of my friends, I have used language stronger than I intended; whereas I have omitted to express myself with emphasis when I have attempted to say good things. Why need I have told of the mud of Washington, or have exposed the nakedness of Cairo? Why did I speak with such eager enmity of those poor women in the New York cars, who never injured me, now that I think of it? Ladies of New York, as I write this, the words which were written among you, are printed and cannot be expunged; but I tender to you my apologies from my home in England.
>
> O, my friends with thin skins, ye whom I call my cousins and love as brethren, will ye not forgive me these harsh words that I have spoken? They have been spoken in love, – with a true love, a brotherly love, a love that has never been absent from the heart while the brain was coining them. I had my task to do, and I could not take the pleasant and ignore the painful. It may perhaps be that as a friend I had better not have written either good or bad. But no! To say that would indeed be to speak calumny of your country. A man may

write of you truly, and yet write that which you would read with pleasure; – only that your skins are so thin! The streets of Washington are muddy and her ways are desolate. The nakedness of Cairo is very naked. And those ladies of New York; is it not to be confessed that they are somewhat imperious in their demands?

A further twenty years did nothing to raise Trollope's opinion of his North American journal: in his autobiography, he described it as 'tedious and confused', concluding, 'I can recommend no one to read it now in order that he may be either instructed or amused'. How many other writers were remorseful, or even aware of the offence they caused, whether in person or in writing? Although most writers, including the Trollopes, found much to praise in America, it was the complaints and the ridicule which were remembered: their irritation, outrage, indignation and frustration brought their written accounts to life. And patriotism – both American and British – gave those paragraphs a power to hurt on one side of the Atlantic, and to amuse on the other. Compliments seemed local, accidental and dull.

A century or more later, these idiosyncratic records of North America can still raise heckles: time has not settled the dispute between two kinds of national arrogance, and two kinds of manners, which see each other as over-formal and over-familiar.

There is one field in which accounts may be assessed more objectively: some of their predictions have now turned out to be right or wrong. Predictions were scattered through every journal, diary and letter, some impressively accurate. In 1869, when the population of California was about half a million, William Fraser Rae wrote that 'within the ample bounds of this large and fertile state 20,000,000 of people can be accommodated with pleasant homes'. The population of California is now more than 23,000,000, the largest in the States.

On the east coast, changes were predicted in the most desirable areas of New York City as a result of the development of Central Park: 'I do not doubt that the present fashion of the Fifth Avenue about Twentieth Street will in course of time move itself up to the Fifth Avenue as it looks, or will look, over the Park at Seventieth, Eightieth, and Ninetieth streets,' wrote Anthony Trollope in 1861. And those streets off Fifth Avenue on the Upper East Side are now among the most expensive in the city.

Of all these writers, the most successful predictions were made by Alexander Mackay, whose pronouncements on long-term changes and influences proved uncannily accurate. 'Twenty years will not elapse ere the Atlantic and Pacific are connected together by a line of railway,' he wrote. Nineteen years after his account was published in 1850, the last spike was driven into a line which connected both coasts, at Promontory Point, Utah, in 1869. Mackay's other predictions were more general, but no less accurate:

Hitherto the Pacific side of America has played but an insignificant part in the commercial and political arrangements of the world. Emigrants are now flocking to it from all quarters; and many years will not elapse ere numerous and energetic communities extend from Vancouver's Island to the head of the Gulf of California.

The west coast of North America has indeed enjoyed an unrivalled prosperity since Mackay wrote those words; its further growth is still predicted as part of the 'Pacific Rim'. Mackay also pronouced on politics:

It is impossible to foresee the changes which may be wrought in habits, tastes, and opinions, during the flight of many succeeding generations; but . . . it will be evident, I think, that for a long time at least, democracy, as the elementary principle of government in America, is sure to maintain itself.

That sentiment was more impressive for being written at a time when many British writers were sceptical about 'the democratic experiment', as they saw it, in the United States.

And, unpatriotically, Mackay predicted that the United States would overtake Britain in prosperity and power; he softened the blow by emphasizing that the British could identify racially with white Americans, and even take a parental pride in American success:

The continent will yet be Anglo-Saxon from Panama to Hudson's Bay. What Anglo-Saxons have done, circumstanced as we have been, is but a faint type of what Anglo-Saxons will yet do, working in far greater numbers, on a far more favourable field of operation.

It is the consideration that America will yet exhibit, in magnified proportions, all that has tended to make England great, that leads one irresistibly, however reluctantly, to the conclusion that the power of England must yet succumb to that of her offspring.

Mackay was right on the economic question; his hope that the British could one day be proud of a larger continent dominated by Anglo-Saxons would, of course, be disputed by a large proportion of today's North Americans.

Other grand predictions were less successful. Anthony Trollope predicted the wrong result of the Civil War:

I cannot believe that the really southern States will ever again be joined in amicable union with those of the North . . . I will not pretend to draw the exact line, or to say how many of them are doomed; but I believe that South Carolina with Georgia, and perhaps five or six others, will be extruded from the Union.

And Charles Weld had an over-optimistic view of the extent of the forest in Canada:

It was ascertained that in the Ottawa forest-region alone there was timber sufficient to feed the mills on that noble river, at their present rate of consumption, for 600 years. A glance at the map of North America shows how small a portion of that vast country is included in this survey; so that, although new channels of communication will be opened into the interior with the extension of commerce, it is not unreasonable to regard the supply of timber as almost inexhaustible.

Captain Marryat, in 1837, realized the population was migrating westward, but dramatically underestimated the extent of its movement:

What will be the consequence when the western states become, as they assuredly will, so populous and powerful as to control the Union? For not only population, but *power* and wealth, are fast working their way to the west. New Orleans will be the first maritime port in the universe, and Cincinnati will not only be the Queen of the West, but Queen of the Western *World*.

Sadly for Cincinnati, the trucks rolled on, further and further west.

Finally, William Fraser Rae generously praised what he believed to be the successful prediction of an older American writer, Richard Dana, about San Francisco:

When Mr. Dana came here in 1835, but a single wooden shanty occupied the site of the present city of San Francisco. As long ago as that year, and when the value of this place had not been ascertained, Mr. Dana made the following entry in the diary, which, under the title of *Two Years before the Mast*, was given to the world in 1840: – 'If California ever becomes a prosperous country, this bay will be the centre of its prosperity. The abundance of wood and water; the extreme fertility of its shores; the excellence of its climate, which is as near to being perfect as any in the world, and its facilities for navigation, affording the best anchoring grounds in the whole western coast of America – all fit it for a place of great importance.' This prediction deserves to be ranked with the most successful specimens of fulfilled prophecy.

Today Rae's tribute to Dana looks unlucky, being caught out by entirely unpredictable influences such as aeroplanes and movies on southern California, where (despite its relative inadequacy as an anchoring ground) the Los Angeles area has become a larger centre of economic activity than San Francisco. Dana had passed Los Angeles, but there was nothing worth stopping for except a few cow-hides, which were thrown down to his ship from the cliffs, and taken back round Cape Horn to Boston to be made into shoe leather for the smart cities of the east coast.

CHAPTER FIFTEEN
HOME AND ABROAD

Many a British tourist can still be heard telling fellow Britons with furrowed brow that America is 'a nice place to visit, but I wouldn't want to live there'. However genuine it may seem, it is not an original thought. Oscar Wilde, with a slight effort to vary the cliché, said that 'though one can dine in New York one could not dwell there'. An early version came from Mrs Trollope, in her remarks about Cincinnati: 'I should have thought it a place delightful to visit, but to tarry there was not to feel at home.' British travellers' comments about America often ended with reminders of home.

Mrs Trollope recommended a trip to the States, but combined faint praise with a strong loyalty to England, whose virtues she believed she could recognize all the more clearly in the light of comparison: she found the States 'a very fine country, well worth visiting for a thousand reasons; nine hundred and ninety-nine of these are reasons founded on admiration and respect; the thousandth is, that we shall feel the more contented with our own'.

For most writers, and surely for Mrs Trollope too, there was more than simple patriotism to draw the thoughts to home. Uncertainty about the present and worry about the future combine to give all travellers, at times, surges of longing for the safety and familiarity of their own country. Robert Louis Stevenson witnessed a powerful outbreak of such feelings on an emigrant train, heading out west:

A man played airs upon the cornet, and none of them were much attended to, until he came to 'Home, Sweet Home.' It was truly strange to note how the talk ceased at that, and the faces began to lengthen. I have no idea whether musically this air is to be considered good or bad; but it belongs to that class of art which may be best described as a brutal assault upon the feelings. Pathos must be relieved by dignity of treatment. If you wallow naked in the pathetic, like the author of 'Home, Sweet Home,' you make your hearers weep in an unmanly fashion; and even while yet they are moved, they despise themselves and hate the occasion of their weakness. It did not come to tears that night, for the experiment was interrupted. An elderly, hard-looking man, with a goatee beard and about as much appearance of sentiment as you would expect from a retired slave, turned with a start and bade the performer stop that 'damned thing.' 'I've heard about enough of that,' he added; 'give us something about the good country we're going to.' A murmur of adhesion ran round the car; the performer took the instrument from his lips, laughed and nodded, and then struck into a dancing measure; and, like a new Timotheus, stilled immediately the emotion he had raised.

For all his travelling, Stevenson himself was a home-lover, declaring that 'the happiest lot on earth is to be born a Scotchman'. He recognized a special bond with his fellow Scots when he met them overseas. Even on honeymoon with his American bride in California, a chance meeting with a fellow Scotsman brought to the surface his feelings for his childhood in Edinburgh:

There is no special loveliness in that grey country, with its rainy, sea-beat archipelago; its fields of dark mountains; its unsightly places, black with coal; its treeless, sour, unfriendly-looking corn-lands; its quaint, grey, castled city, where the bells clash of a Sunday, and the wind squalls, and the salt showers fly and beat. I do not even know if I desire to live there; but let me hear, in some far land, a kindred voice sing out, 'Oh, why left I my hame?' and it seems at once as if no beauty under the kind heavens, and no society of the wise and good, can repay me for my absence from my country. And though I think I would rather die elsewhere, yet in my heart of hearts I long to be buried among good Scots clods.

For many emigrants, this was an abiding question: could they, in the end, transfer allegiance from their home of birth to their country of adoption? Here were the deepest, saddest feelings, as Catherine Parr Traill recalled:

I called, one day, while in the Bush, at the house of a venerable old man of eighty – a soldier and a gentleman – who had been here forty years, and seldom got any tidings from home. I happened to have in my pocket-book a primrose, which dearest — sent me in a letter, and I placed it on the old man's knee and said, 'Did you ever see a flower like that?' The old man took it up and when he recognised it he kissed the pale flower over and over again, and bending his aged head he wept like a child, so long and so violently that I was alarmed. Who can tell what thoughts this little flower awakened in the old man's mind? The thoughts of some shady lane perchance, near the unforgotten home of his childhood, 'The first love-beat of his youthful heart,' a mother's gentle look, a father's word of approbation, or sign of reproof; a sister's gentle love, a brother's fond regard, handsful of flowers plucked in green and quiet meadows – birds' nests admired, but not touched – the Sabbath call to prayer and praise. It was too sacred a sight for a stranger's eye. I don't *think* he could have spoken, I am sure I could not. So I wrote in pencil a few words promising to see him again, and, if we should be both spared, that he should next spring, have a pale memorial of spring and home from the same green lane as the one which had, much to his honour, elicited, 'A Soldier's Tear.'

For Traill, this was an unaccustomed, if vicarious, admission of such strong emotions. Her staunch, practical approach to the settler's life did not allow for too much reflection on the past, or distant England. Less than three years after emigrating, she noted in her journal that 'it has ever been my way to extract the sweet rather than the bitter in the cup of life, and surely it is best and wisest so to do'. Yet this optimism seemed to veil only thinly a layer of struggle, both physical and emotional:

> In a country where constant exertion is called for from all ages and degrees of settlers, it would be foolish to a degree to damp our energies by complaints, and cast a gloom over our homes by sitting dejectedly down to lament for all that was so dear to us in the old country . . . My husband is becoming more reconciled to the country, and I daily feel my attachment to it strengthening. The very stumps that appeared so odious, through long custom seem to lose some of their hideousness; the eye becomes familiarized even with objects the most displeasing till they cease to be observed.

Traill's sister, Susanna Moodie, wrote a more personal account of her own emigration, and her feelings during the first months and years in Canada. In the early days, her homesickness was acute:

> My whole soul yielded itself up to a strong and overpowering grief. One simple word dwelt for ever in my heart, and swelled it to bursting – 'Home!' I repeated it waking a thousand times a day, and my last prayer before I sank to sleep was still 'Home! Oh that I could return, if only to die at home!' And nightly I did return; my feet trod the daisied meadows of England; the song of her birds was in my ears; I wept with delight to find myself once more wandering beneath the fragrant shade of her green hedge-rows; and I awoke to weep in earnest when I found it but a dream.

Moodie wrote of the 'blinding tears' which prevented her reading the first letters which arrived from home. But, looking back on her early years in Canada, she chronicled the declining passion of her correspondence: after seven years 'letters grow fewer and colder, their expressions of attachment are less vivid; the heart has formed new ties, and the poor emigrant is nearly forgotten'. In fourteen years, 'it is as if the grave had closed over you, and the hearts that once knew and loved you know you no more'. In a later book, written over two decades after emigration, Moodie was able to conclude, triumphantly, of Canada, 'I no longer regard myself as an alien on her shores, but her daughter by adoption, – the happy mother of Canadian children, – rejoicing in the warmth and hospitality of a Canadian Home!'

Those who were only visiting North America had no need to make the long emotional journey of the emigrant. And yet, in a few weeks or months, they too could experience a sadness at being, as Anna Brownell Jameson said, 'a stranger among strangers'. Many a British traveller longed for what Isabella Bird, writing with freezing ink in a Colorado winter, described as 'the quietness and purity of English domestic life'. Charles Kingsley loved all he found in egalitarian America, but revealed his true loyalties when he wrote to his wife from California: 'tell all the servants I wish heartily I was through and safe home again, for there is no place like England.'

But just before embarking on the journey home, some of these temporary visitors, many of whom had written severely about aspects of life in North America, found themselves overtaken with a wave of affection, not for home, but for what they were leaving. Charles Dickens wrote warmly of his departure from New York:

> I never thought that going back to England, returning to all who are dear to me, and to pursuits that have insensibly grown to be a part of my nature, I could have felt so much sorrow as I endured, when I parted at last, on board this ship, with the friends who had accompanied me from this city. I never thought the name of any place, so far away and so lately known, could ever associate itself in my mind with the crowd of affectionate remembrances that now cluster about it. There are those in this city who would brighten, to me, the darkest winter-day that ever glimmered and went out in Lapland; and before whose presence even Home grew dim.

Even the relentlessly jovial Captain Horton Rhys allowed himself a spluttering departure speech:

> *Farewell*, I did not imagine the amount of regret I should feel – yes, real, unfeigned regret . . . an indescribable – sort of clinging, sad-to-part-with-feeling, that no one – at least, I don't know anyone that can put on to paper!

Anthony Trollope took his leave gracefully:

> When the snow went in Boston I went with it. The evening before I left I watched them as they carted away the dirty uncouth blocks which had been broken up with pickaxes in Washington Street, and was melancholy as I reflected that I too should no longer be known in the streets. My weeks in Boston had not been very many, but nevertheless there were haunts there which I knew as though my feet had trodden them for years.

'If any English person can really see and know the Americans on their own ground, and fail to honour them as a nation, and love them as personal friends, he is no fair sample of the people whose name he bears.'
                                                                HARRIET MARTINEAU

It was a time for generosity, for saying those things which detailed criticisms might not have let the reader assume; most British visitors had much to remember fondly about the Americans. Dickens paid a handsome tribute:

> They are, by nature, frank, brave, cordial, hospitable, and affectionate. Cultivation and refinement seem but to enhance their warmth of heart and ardent enthusiasm; and it is the possession of these latter qualities in a most remarkable degree, which renders an educated American one of the most endearing and most generous of friends. I never was so won upon, as by this class; never yielded up my full confidence and esteem so readily and

pleasurably, as to them; never can make again, in half a year, so many friends for whom I seem to entertain the regard of half a life.

Dickens wrote warmly of Canada too, 'health and vigour throbbing in its steady pulse; it is full of hope and promise'.

Others shared such affectionate feelings:

It is not so much the outward plenty, or the mutual freedom, or the simplicity of manners, or the incessant play of humour, which characterise the whole people, as the sweet temper which is diffused like sunshine over the land. They have been called the most good-tempered people in the world: and I think they must be so.

HARRIET MARTINEAU

I think there is no one in the world so hospitable and kind as the American gentleman: whether in the Eastern or Western states, it is just the same – the same courtesy and kindness, the same readiness to be of any help or service to the stranger who is fortunate enough to be possessed of an introduction to him, always distinguish him. We had some difficulty parting with our kind friends, so pressing was their hospitality.

W. HENRY BARNEBY

Even some of the Americans' most criticized habits could be seen in a better light, as R. Byron Johnson noticed:

People talk a good deal of the impertinent curiosity displayed by our trans-Atlantic cousins, but I think there is more of the kindly feeling . . . actuating them than aught else. Moreover their manner is genial, and their curiosity does not usually take an offensive turn; and it is certain that when the Englishman's reserve once wears off, he is always one of the strongest advocates of a freer intercourse among people thrown together in a casual way.

James Dixon managed to describe as virtues most of the traits which the British usually abhorred:

It is refreshing even to look upon a true and real American, with his swinging gait, in the full consciousness of his manhood. There is something even in his appearance different from other people. It is not recklessness, not rudeness, not isolation, not misanthropy. Nothing of this sort is seen. And yet there is an air of perfect independence and freedom, consciousness of strength and power, repose in the midst of activity, calmness and dignity with profound emotions. An American, more than any character it was ever my happiness to study, looks like a man who is sensible that he carries his own destinies about him; that he is complete in himself; that he is a self-acting, self-moving intelligence; that he has to shape his own course, and become the architect of his fortune. He does not seem to be looking without to catch the chances of some stray events by which to fashion his life: his thoughts are steadily fixed upon strengthening his own resources, and he is always laying in a stock for the voyage he is upon. The effect of this is to produce (I hardly know what to call it) a rotundity, a fulness, a completeness of manhood, not seen in other societies; and to those who do not comprehend him, or who have only been accustomed to the fawning flatteries – and as false as they are fawning – of other nations, all this is extremely offensive.

And there was even an occasional cheer for the much-derided political philosophy of the United States. Oscar Wilde concluded his *Impressions of America* with a bold claim:

The Americans are the best politically educated people in the world. It is well worth one's while to go to a country which can teach us the beauty of the word FREEDOM and the value of the thing LIBERTY.

Barbara Bodichon excused a certain 'careworn' look of Americans as being 'because they all feel so intensely the responsibility of government'. She too had learnt to recognize and appreciate a new atmosphere:

I find myself saying continually, 'This is a free country.' One is so little used to freedom, real freedom, even in England that it takes time to understand freedom, to realize it. Nothing sent from upper powers to be worshipped or humbly listened to, no parsons sent by a class of born rulers to preach and lecture to another class born to submit and pay. No race of men with honours they have not earned and power over others which the others have not consented them! Heavens, what a difference! Here all who hold power are heaved up by the people, of the people. Until I came to America I hardly felt the strange want of rational liberty in England. How came Franklin and Washington to dare to try this huge experiment? Why, because they saw it was right.

No British travellers went so far as to claim they preferred North America to Britain, although there was sometimes a hint that Britain was not always best: 'I was frequently forced to admit,' wrote Edward Sullivan, 'that though we do most things well in England, yet that they do some things even better in America.' Bertrand Russell found that 'against my will, in the course of my travels, the belief that everything worth knowing was known at Cambridge, gradually wore off'.

'The more unlike a country through which we travel is to all we have left, the more we are likely to be amused.'
FANNY TROLLOPE

Some were unrepentant. Mrs Trollope acknowledged that she had met people in America 'whom I love and admire, far beyond the love and admiration of ordinary acquaintance', but remained adamant in her views about the mass of the population: 'I do not like them. I do not like their principles. I do not like their manners, I do not like their opinions.'

After recrossing the Atlantic, returning visitors from North America find that for a few days, familiar sights are no longer absolutes, but comparatives: their home has become a novelty, to be measured against the patterns of the United States and Canada. Anthony Trollope's steamer to Liverpool first stopped at Queenstown, near Cork, in Ireland. Trollope, who had lived in Ireland, immediately saw the usual crowds of beggars clamouring for money, through the eyes of Americans: 'what would those Americans think of them; – of them and of the country which produced them? That was the reflection which troubled me.'

The bigger, young continent shows Britain as smaller and older than it once appeared to the traveller. But familiarity soon returns, and excuses many defects of scale and affluence: this is home. Dickens, on a train back to London, surveyed the landscape with fresh eyes, but his heart had no reservations about England or its people:

The country, by the railroad, seemed, as we rattled through it, like a luxuriant garden. The beauty of the fields (so small they looked!), the hedge-rows, and the trees; the pretty cottages, the beds of flowers, the old churchyards, the antique houses, and every well-known object; the exquisite delights of that one journey, crowding in the short compass of a summer's day, the joy of many years, and winding up with Home and all that makes it dear; no tongue can tell, or pen of mine describe.

APPENDIX ONE

THE WRITERS AND THEIR JOURNEYS

MATTHEW ARNOLD (1822–88), the poet, educationalist and critic, undertook two lecture tours of America in 1883–4, and in 1886, both when he was over sixty. He travelled as far as St Louis, reporting that as he went further west he began 'to recognize the truth of what an American told the Bishop of Rochester, that "Denver was not ripe for Mr Arnold"'. He was critical of many aspects of life in America, but enjoyed the more sedate pace of the south.

W. HENRY BARNEBY from Herefordshire, travelled to the States and Canada in 1883, with his friend Meysey Clive, and his brother-in-law, Arthur Mitchell. Their journey was both for pleasure, and to collect information for those hoping to emigrate. The party travelled across Canada to British Columbia, and as far south in California as Los Angeles. But Clive became ill and died, bringing the trip to a premature end. Barneby's account, written in letters home to his wife, was transcribed by her, ready for publication as *Life and Labour in the Far, Far West* (1884) on his return.

ISABELLA BIRD – *see* p. 58

BARBARA BODICHON (1827–91) was the oldest of five illegitimate children of a radical Liberal MP. Her father sent her to Algeria with three of her sisters, to help her forget a love affair with a married man. There she met, and later married, a French doctor, Eugène Bodichon. The couple set off on their American travels in 1857, a few weeks after the wedding. Mrs Bodichon was a painter, feminist, writer, and friend of many well-known figures of her time, including George Eliot and John Ruskin. She campaigned for university education for women, and was instrumental in the founding of Girton College, Cambridge. Her American diary is much concerned with observing slavery during an extensive tour of the south. She was fascinated by America, but not attracted to it: 'I shall never come to America again,' she wrote, 'never as long as I live, I hope. I do not like it well enough. Though it is more worth seeing than all other countries.'

GEORGE TUTHILL BORRETT, a Fellow of King's College, Cambridge, travelled round Canada and the northern states in 1864, publishing his letters as a book on his return to his home in London.

CLARA FITZROY BROMLEY visited North and South America, including Mexico and the Caribbean in 1853–4. The trip was undertaken 'for the renovation of health and spirits, severely shaken by domestic losses during the preceding year'. She was accompanied by a young female friend, and reported that over 20,000 miles and ten months she 'met with no word or act of annoyance from first to last'. Her letters home to her father were published as *A Woman's Wanderings in the Western World* (1861).

REBECCA BURLAND (1793–1872) and her husband, together with two of their five children, sailed from Liverpool to New Orleans, and thence up the Mississippi to set up home in Pike County, Illinois. After years of labour and set-backs, the family became prosperous enough for Mrs Burland to revisit England to see her children and friends. She told her story to her son, Edward, a poet and schoolteacher. He wrote it up as *A True Picture of Emigration; Or Fourteen Years in the Interior of North America; Being a Full and Impartial Account of the Various Difficulties and Ultimate Success of an English Family Who Emigrated from Barwick-In-Elmet, Near Leeds, in the Year 1831* (1848). Mrs Burland returned to Illinois accompanied by one of her daughters and the daughter's family. Burland advised future emigrants that 'if our success has been ultimately greater than at one time we anticipated, or even than that of many of our neighbours, as indeed it has, it must be borne in mind that our industry and perseverance have been unremitting'.

SIR RICHARD FRANCIS BURTON (1821–90) was a remarkable scholar and explorer. He mastered over thirty languages, and travelled the world, writing more than fifty books of travel, novels and translations. His visit to the States in 1860 took him to Salt Lake City, to report on the Mormons, and to California.

MRS E.H. CARBUTT visited America in 1888 to enjoy, as her account was titled, *Five Months' Fine Weather in Canada, Western U.S., and Mexico* (1889). Accompanied by her husband, Edward, she completed an extensive itinerary, including southern California.

WILLIAM COBBETT (1762–1835) first went to North America as a British soldier, spending nine years in eastern Canada, in Nova Scotia and New Brunswick. He returned to England and left the army. In 1792 he returned to America, settling in Philadelphia, where he opened a bookshop and wrote political commentary under the name of Peter Porcupine. In trouble for libel, he returned to England in 1800. In 1817 he visited the States a third time, to farm in Long Island, New York. He chronicled his experience in *A Year's Residence in the United States of America* (1819). The book is a detailed guide for immigrant farmers, containing extensive instructions, for instance, on the cultivation of the Swedish turnip. Cobbett concluded that the idea of equality between United States citizens made for 'a country of *universal civility*'. He returned to England, and published his most famous work, *Rural Rides* (1830).

CHARLES DICKENS – *see p. 9*

JAMES DIXON (1788–1871) was a well-known Wesleyan preacher who visited the United States in 1848 to represent English Methodists at a church conference in Pittsburgh. He gathered information about Methodism in the States, and in Canada, where he presided over another conference at Belleville, Ontario. His *Personal Narrative* (1849) of his tour touched on many secular matters, and included a severe criticism of his fellow British writers, whose accounts of America, he believed, were narrow-minded and petty in their complaints: 'Of what consequence can it be to the morality, the honour, the greatness of a people, that they should fashion their course by adopting the manners of the most frivolous, useless, and unreal portions of our own people?'

HENRY BRADSHAW FEARON was commissioned by thirty-nine English families to explore the United States in search of the best area for emigration. He travelled, in 1817–18, to New York, Boston, Philadelphia, Pittsburgh, and into Ohio and Kentucky. He made arrangements to buy land for himself in Illinois, and offered a qualified recommendation to his fellow countrymen to follow him, warning every emigrant that 'he must not expect to find either the country full of gold, or its inhabitants as agreeable or as sociable as the perhaps unequalled people of England'.

REVD ISAAC FIDLER was an Anglican minister who travelled to the United States and Canada in 1831. He found a ministry in a small town near Toronto (or York as it then was), but his wife insisted they should return to England. He strongly advised emigrants to choose Canada rather than the States, because, he claimed, in the States, British settlers would find themselves 'among a people of different habits and different sentiments from themselves, in Canada they are among their own countrymen'.

LADY THEODORA GUEST enjoyed the fastest and most comfortable journey of all these travellers; in 1895 she and her party had their own railway carriage, complete with staff, which made a 10,000 mile round-trip, taking in Washington, San Francisco and Toronto in only six weeks. She mixed in the highest circles, but seemed more interested in the flora and fauna than the people. If there was time to stop anywhere she would sketch, while her husband went in search of photographic shops from which to buy souvenirs of local sights. She concluded about her journey: 'No wonder we were sorry it was over! Nowhere but in America can one experience such luxury.'

CAPTAIN BASIL HALL (1788–1844), a much-travelled British naval officer, toured America with his wife, Margaret, and daughter, Eliza, who was only fourteen months old at the start of the trip in 1827. His survey of North American society and institutions was based on personal observation; he had avoided reading accounts of similar tours, and claimed he was not well read on other subjects either. Nevertheless, his three-volume report is both colourful in its descriptions of society and manners, and detailed in its pictures of institutions such as prisons and schools. He travelled north into the backwoods of Canada, and south to Alabama to observe slavery, as well as taking in the usual sights of the east coast. His trip was cut short in its second year by the illness of his daughter, whose successful treatment for cholera, at the recommendation of a local doctor, was a swift departure from the Mississippi basin up into the healthier atmosphere of the Allegheny mountains east of Pittsburgh. Published three years before Mrs Trollope's book, Hall's *Travels in North America* (1829) was one of the earliest and most widely read of these journals.

THOMAS HAMILTON (1789–1842) was an army officer, who settled in Edinburgh on his retirement, and turned to writing. His novel, *Cyril Thornton* (1827), was popular on both sides of the Atlantic. He travelled to the United States and wrote an extensive report, *Men and Manners in America* (1833). Hamilton described the customs of America with a wry humour, but was dismissive of many achievements, including the American government: 'I have never yet met with any man in this country whose opinions could carry with them any weight, who was not decidedly of opinion that the system of government here is in many respects a *decided failure*.'

SIR FRANCIS BOND HEAD (1793–1875) was a traveller, industrialist and writer. He was an unpopular Governor of Upper Canada from 1835 to 1837, but wrote about ordinary life in the country in a series of light essays collected together as *The Emigrant* (1846).

ANNA BROWNELL JAMESON (1794–1860) went to Canada in 1836 to join her husband, who had been appointed Attorney-General of Ontario. She thoroughly disliked Toronto's winter climate, and its society, which she saw as petty and provincial. A visit to Niagara Falls proved another disappointment, as was her marriage. When the spring came, she left her husband to go on a trip through Ontario to Detroit, then north to visit the Indians around Sault Ste Marie and Manitoulin Island in Lake Huron. She travelled across the lake in a canoe paddled by French-Canadian voyageurs, camping on uninhabited islands: 'I cannot, I dare not, attempt to describe to you the strange sensation one has, thus thrown for a time beyond the bounds of civilised humanity; nor the wild yet solemn reveries which come over one in the midst of this wilderness of woods and waters.' She returned to Toronto after two months, completed legal arrangements to separate from her husband, and returned to London, via Boston, where she stayed for a time with her friend Fanny Kemble. She was the author of several books on literature and travel before she published her Canadian experiences as *Winter Studies and Summer Rambles in Canada* (1838).

R. BYRON JOHNSON sailed from Southampton in 1862, seeking his fortune in the goldfields of British Columbia. After a series of adventures in San Francisco, Victoria, and the interior of British Columbia, Johnson discovered that prospecting was not an easy way to riches, although he did have some luck, and persistence eventually made him, as he said, 'a man of modest capital'. Advising others on the attractions of emigrating, he stressed the importance of three qualities, 'Brains, Money, and Muscle'. And on British Columbia, he concluded, 'I don't think it a place for a delicate person to go to'.

FANNY KEMBLE – *see* p. 103

CHARLES KINGSLEY (1819–75), the essayist and novelist, author of *Westward Ho!* (1855) and *The Water-Babies* (1863), visited the United States and Canada with his daughter, Rose, in 1874, the year before he died. Kingsley was well known, and found himself a celebrated literary figure in the cities he visited, and a guest of President Grant in Washington. His tour took him to San Francisco, where he talked to students at Berkeley University. The student newspaper recorded that 'a speech so invigorating, and yet so simple, will be long remembered – like a draught of pure water in a thirsty clime'. Although Kingsley never wrote a book about his travels, his letters, published posthumously by his wife, record his enthusiasm for the United States: 'it is a glorious country, and I don't wonder at the people being proud of it.'

RUDYARD KIPLING (1856–1936) had been living and working as a journalist in India, when he crossed America in 1889, on his way to England, where he established a new life in London. Three years later he married Caroline Balestier, an American, and the couple lived for a time near her family in Vermont. There he wrote *The Jungle Books* (1894 and 1895). His experience of America gave him material for work such as *Captains Courageous* (1897), written after the Kiplings had returned to England. He returned to Vermont in 1898 to sell his property. Kipling's American travel writing was collected in *From Sea to Sea* (1899). It chronicled his adventurous journey across the continent a decade earlier. He found that his own enthusiasm for America ('let there be no misunderstanding about the matter. I love this People') was exceeded only by that of its inhabitants, whom he wanted to remind that 'America is a very great country, but it is not yet Heaven with electric lights'. He returned to Canada in 1907, revisiting some of the places he had seen on his earlier travels, and recorded his observations in *Letters to the Family (Notes on a recent trip to Canada)* (1908).

JOHN LANGTON (1808–94) and ANNE LANGTON (1804–93) emigrated from near Liverpool to Ontario in the 1830s. John was a young barrister when he decided to take a chance on buying land in the backwoods, and setting up a farm in Canada. Four years after his arrival in Canada, his older sister, Anne, came to join him, together with their parents. Both Anne and John lived to their eighties, John having become a Member of Parliament, and Auditor General of Canada. His letters home to his father, before the rest of the family had joined him, were published as *Early Days in Upper Canada* (1926); Anne's letters and journals were collected as *A Gentlewoman in Upper Canada* (1950).

ALEXANDER MACKAY (1808–52) was a London barrister who toured the United States in 1846 and 1847 to produce a three-volume account of the country's development. He enjoyed the relaxed hospitality of wealthy, southern families, which he compared to that of the great English country houses, and contrasted with the mercantile life in the northern cities. He was positive in his assessments, blaming other British writers for 'caricaturing' Americans, and advising his fellow visitors: 'be frank, fair, and honest with them, treating them not with marked deference, but with ordinary courtesy, and a more kind-hearted, accessible, hospitable and manageable people are not to be found.'

CHARLES MACKAY (1814–89) was a journalist, poet, and songwriter. He visited America in 1857–8 on a lecture tour, collecting his reports together when he returned as *Life and Liberty in America* (1859).

CAPTAIN FREDERICK MARRYAT (1792–1848) is best known as the author of *Mr Midshipman Easy* (1836) and over thirty other novels, including children's books such as *Children of the New Forest* (1847). He was a naval officer until his late thirties, when he began to write. Ten years later he went to North America, hoping to produce the definitive account of its government and society. His reputation in the United States suffered after he became embroiled in an incident between a group of Canadian loyalists and some Canadian rebels and their

American supporters. Reports that he supported the loyalists led to his books being burned in the United States, together with his effigy. Marryat cut short his trip, but still managed to produce six volumes on his experiences, some in diary form and others containing a series of essays on subjects such as language, religion and women. There was enough to please America in Marryat's account to allow the *New York Review* to describe it as 'very entertaining . . . we like the general spirit of the work'. But on his central inquiry, with hindsight, Marryat's judgements look less impressive: he concluded about its political system, that the United States 'has proved to the world that with every advantage on her side, the attempt at a republic has been a miserable failure, and that the time is not yet come when mankind can govern themselves. Will it ever come? In my opinion, never!'

HARRIET MARTINEAU (1802–76) began writing on religion, but added economics, fiction and travel to the fields in which her work was known and respected. She visited the United States in 1834, and wrote copiously about her experiences in *Society in America* (1837) and *A Retrospect of Western Travel* (1838). She encouraged mutual respect between Britain and America, concluding that 'if any English person can really see and know the Americans on their own ground, and fail to honour them as a nation, and love them as personal friends, he is no fair sample of the people whose name he bears'.

SARAH MYTTON MAURY was the wife of an American cotton-trader who had settled in Liverpool. Mrs Maury travelled to America in 1845, and returned with an uncritical account of slavery, whose practice had made her husband's fortune. She met many of the country's top politicians, whose stories she told in *The Statesmen of America* (1847), before publishing her own account of *An Englishwoman in America* (1848).

SUSANNA MOODIE – *see* p. 77

HON. AMELIA M. MURRAY (1795–1884) visited Canada, the United States and Cuba in 1854–5, without, she claimed, intending to write an account of her visit. Her letters, published the year after her return to England, were noted for their pro-slavery views, which were specifically refuted by Barbara Bodichon, among others. Murray evidently guessed that her opinions would be unpopular, pleading in the book's preface that the author had no wish to enter into controversy, 'however different her convictions may be from the opinions commonly maintained'.

THOMAS NEED went to Oxford, and then decided to emigrate to Canada in 1832, where he bought 3,000 acres of uncleared forest in Ontario for a dollar an acre (each acre, he helpfully noted, costing about the same as a bottle of wine). His experiences at university were only marginally useful for his life in the Bush: a few afternoons of rowing on the 'still surface of the Isis' were, he found, 'a very different affair from encountering a head wind and a heavy sea on a Canadian lake'. He was a neighbour and contemporary of the Langtons, in whose journal he featured, described in a letter from Mrs Langton to her son in England: 'he is in our opinion one of the most agreeable of the young men, though his appearance is less prepossessing than that of some of the others.' Need made enough money to construct a profitable saw-mill, which gave him the means to visit England and arrange for the publication of his backwoods' journal. It was read with interest by his Canadian neighbours: Anne Langton commented to her brother in England: 'it is a slight affair to have attracted so much notice . . . I think he has been well-paid for the trouble of putting it together – it is something of a puff.' Need inherited money from an aunt, and returned permanently to England twelve years after arriving in Canada.

TYRONE POWER (1797–1841) was an Irish actor, who toured America from 1833 to 1835. His *Impressions of America* (1836) found much to praise, including America's reception of Irish immigrants, whose behaviour Power felt obliged to defend: 'let it not be considered an unpardonable enormity that the poor Irishman runs a little riot when suddenly and wholly freed from the heavy clog by which exhibition of his opinions has been restrained at home.'

WILLIAM FRASER RAE (1835–1905) travelled from New York to San Francisco by rail in 1869, the year in which connection was made between tracks from the east and west coasts. Rae was an English journalist, who sent back reports to *The Daily News* before they were collected and expanded to form *Westward by Rail* (1870). He found that although the American press was often virulently anti-British, people he met were the opposite: 'nothing gratified me more than the feeling of kindliness towards the Old Country which I found pervading the American people.'

CAPTAIN CHARLES HORTON RHYS was an unusual traveller, his trip being the result of a bet undertaken to prove that he could earn a living from amateur acting. He went on tour in the United States and Canada in 1859 (a condition of the bet being that his audience must not know of him, or know he was an amateur). Accompanied by a female assistant, Rhys, under the pseudonym of Morton Price, succeeded in his task, and, as a bonus, wrote an entertaining account of his tour, *A Theatrical Trip for a Wager* (1861).

J. EWING RITCHIE travelled across Canada in 1884, meeting up with his old childhood friends from Suffolk, Susanna Moodie, and her sister, Catherine Parr Traill, at their homes in Ontario. Ritchie had remained in England, but he too was a prolific writer, specializing in history books.

EDWARD ROPER, a Fellow of the Royal Geographical Society, travelled across Canada in 1888, publishing his account of the trip as *By Track and Trail – A Journey through Canada* (1891), complete with his own illustrations.

BERTRAND RUSSELL (1872–1970), the English philosopher, married an American, Alys Pearsall Smith, and combined a visit to her family in 1896 with a lecture tour of universities. Russell referred to America in his *Autobiography* (1967) as 'a curiously innocent country', particularly among the old and traditional Quaker families of Philadelphia, where he found his wife's aunt 'very rich and very absurd'.

WILLIAM SHAW, a self-confesssed gold-seeker, described his adventures on the west coast of America and in the Pacific Islands as *Golden Dreams and Waking Realities* (1851).

ROBERT LOUIS STEVENSON – *see* p. 41

EDWARD SULLIVAN crossed the Atlantic in 1850, and published his *Rambles and Scrambles in North and South America* two years later. Although his writing appears casual, with an appetite for the dramatic, he was often astute in his assessments: 'The Americans are essentially a practical people,' he wrote, 'and make every use of the progressive improvements of the age.'

WILLIAM MAKEPEACE THACKERAY (1811–63), novelist, author of *Vanity Fair* (1847), visited the United States for two sets of lecture tours, in 1851–3 and 1855–6. *The Virginians* (1857), set partly in America, was one of the results of his travels. Thackeray was extraordinarily callous about slavery, his letters from the southern states being full of jokes and ridicule of the black population: 'they are not my fellow men and bretheren.'

WILLIAM THOMSON was a textile worker from near Aberdeen. He was advised by his doctor to find a warmer climate, and so visited his two brothers who were living in South Carolina. He then decided to travel and work his way around the continent, a three-year trip he recounted in *A Tradesman's Travels* (1842).

CATHERINE PARR TRAILL – *see* p. 78

ANTHONY TROLLOPE – *see* p. 21

FANNY TROLLOPE – *see* p. 172

ISABELLA (STRANGE) TROTTER (1816–78) toured America with her father in 1858, publishing her account, *First Impressions of the New World on Two Travellers from the Old*, anonymously, the following year on her return to England.

CHARLES RICHARD WELD (1813–69) was a London barrister, whose *Vacation Tour in the United States and Canada* (1855) was one of a series of books he wrote about different countries. Weld was particularly interested in North America because his older half-brother, Isaac, had written a book about a similar tour he had made in the 1790s. *Vacation Tour* was well received in London, one reviewer commenting that it contained 'no unnecesary flattery of the American people, and no bigotted detraction'.

OSCAR WILDE (1854–1900) was a celebrated aesthete in London when Gilbert and Sullivan's *Patience* (1881) mocked the styles for which he was famous. He went to New York on a lecture tour in 1882 at the instigation of the producers of *Patience* in New York, who thought his arrival would be useful publicity for their production. Wilde lectured on house decoration and 'the English Renaissance'. He was elated at the jubilant reception he received in America, boasting in a letter home that he was being treated like the Prince of Wales. The following year, he attended the New York opening of his play *Vera*, but it was not well received. He later wrote two essays, *Impressions of America* (1883) and *The American Invasion* (1887), an amusing account of young American women in London.

FRANCES WRIGHT (1795–1852) arrived in America in 1818, aged twenty-three, with her sister, Camilla. She had already studied all she could about the United States from her home in Scotland, and was inspired by the political ideals of the country. Two years later, the sisters returned to Scotland, where Wright revised her letters written during the tour, and published them as *Views of Society and Manners in America* (1821). The book was attacked by conservatives for its sympathetic treatment of American ideas, but it gave Wright an acquaintance with leading British and European radicals. She returned to America in 1824 on a visit which tempered her enthusiasm with distress at the slavery she saw in the southern states. In an attempt to improve the lot of slaves, she set up a community in Tennessee, and persuaded Mrs Trollope to join her there. The project ultimately failed, but Wright moved to New York to campaign on social issues. 'Fanny Wrightism' became a term for radical ideas. She died in Cincinnati, somewhat forgotten by society, in 1852.

APPENDIX TWO

CHRONOLOGY OF VISITS AND CURRENT EVENTS

Writer	date arrived	current events
William Cobbett	1817	1817: Construction begins on the Erie Canal, linking Great Lakes to the Atlantic
Henry Bradshaw Fearon	1817	
Frances Wright	1818	1820: US population – 10 million
		1825: First railway service opens, in England
Fanny Trollope	1827	
Basil Hall	1827	
		1830: First settlers' wagon trains cross the Rockies
Rebecca Burland	1831	
Revd Isaac Fidler	1831	
Fanny Kemble	1832	1832: Great Reform Bill in Britain
Susanna Moodie	1832	
Thomas Need	1832	
Catherine Parr Traill	1832	
Thomas Hamilton	1833	1833: Founding of Chicago
John Langton	1833	
Tyrone Power	1833	
Harriet Martineau	1834	1834: End of slavery in British colonies
Sir Francis Bond Head	1835	
Anna Brownell Jameson	1836	
Anne Langton	1837	1837: Start of Queen Victoria's reign
Captain Frederick Marryat	1837	
		1839: First British steamship service across the Atlantic
William Thomson	1840	
		1841: Proclamation of Union of Upper and Lower Canada
Charles Dickens	1842	
		1844: Samuel Morse invents the telegraph
Sarah Mytton Maury	1845	
Alexander Mackay	1846	1846: United States declares war on Mexico

Writer	date arrived	current events
James Dixon	1848	1848: Gold discovered in California
William Shaw	1849	
Edward Sullivan	1850	1850: California joins United States, 31st state in Union
William Makepeace Thackeray	1851	1851: Great Exhibition, in London
Clara Fitzroy Bromley	1853	
Amelia M. Murray	1854	1854: Crimean War
Isabella Bird	1854	
Charles Weld	1855	
Barbara Bodichon	1857	
Charles Mackay	1857	
Isabella Strange Trotter	1858	1858: First trans-Atlantic telegraph cable laid. Ottawa selected as capital of Canada
Captain Horton Rhys	1859	
Sir Richard Burton	1860	1860: Southern states secede from Union
Anthony Trollope	1861	1861: Abraham Lincoln becomes President; outbreak of Civil War
R. Byron Johnson	1862	
		1863: Lincoln issues Emancipation Proclamation
George Tuthill Borrett	1864	
		1867: Dominion of Canada Act – Quebec and Nova Scotia join
William Fraser Rae	1869	1869: Completion of first transcontinental railway
		1870: British Columbia joins Confederation of Canada
		1873: First cable cars in San Francisco
Charles Kingsley	1874	
		1876: Alexander Graham Bell demonstrates telephone in Boston
Robert Louis Stevenson	1879	1879: Thomas Edison invents electric light bulb
Oscar Wilde	1882	
Matthew Arnold	1883	1883: Completion of Brooklyn Bridge
W. Henry Barneby	1883	
J. Ewing Ritchie	1884	
		1886: Canadian-Pacific railway completed
Mrs E.H. Carbutt	1888	
Edward Roper	1888	
Rudyard Kipling	1889	
		1890: Battle of Wounded Knee
Lady Theodora Guest	1895	
Bertrand Russell	1896	
		1898: United States annexes Hawaii

194

APPENDIX THREE

BRITISH IMPRESSIONS OF AMERICA, PAST AND PRESENT

While nineteenth-century British visitors found North American society casual and unstructured, typically complaining that nobody 'knew their place', today social rules in America seem stronger than in Britain. The British now often comment that Americans have beautiful 'manners', a term which is otherwise rarely used. Undoubtedly, personal manners are better in America, in the sense of being more closely defined and observed. And social codes are stricter: whether on questions of driving or parking, tipping, or dress and make-up, North America seems to have a higher expectation of conformity. Identification with their culture and its demands is attested by the unselfconscious patriotism of Americans and Canadians; in Britain, national pride is subverted by an upper-class nostalgia, or laddish jingoism. Although the North American cultures promise free choice on almost any question, the unconventional is rarely chosen. Britain has become the nation of individuals, now closely packed on a small island, and each living in a self-made cultural world.

One of the other great themes of the nineteenth century, democracy in the United States, is more potent and popular an idea than ever: an essay in America's *Newsweek* magazine by Joe Klein (12 July 1993) discussed alternative political systems which might better suit developing countries, but remained confident in its basic assumption that 'obviously, no intellectual challenge to democracy can be all that strong'. While that has been the attitude of Americans since the last century, today commentators from almost every other country enthusiastically embrace the principles (if not always the particular expressions) of the American political system.

Some of the more specific British observations of the last century can still be heard today: America's supposedly blasé attitude to death was once more remarked upon by Phil Reeves in Britain's *Independent* newspaper (18 August 1993). Reeves described how he flagged down a police car when he saw a man lying on a Washington pavement one morning: 'the officer slowly eased his bulk out of the car and sauntered over to the body with a seen-it-all done-it-all swagger . . . By now a small crowd had gathered. It was impossible not to notice that they, too, lacked any apparent concern. There were no cries for a doctor, no concerned questions about the whereabouts of the ambulance.'

British judgments about American language continue to provoke trans-Atlantic indignation: William Safire (*New York Times*, 22 August 1993) complained about the tone of 'unmistakable disdain' in a British Broadcasting Corporation booklet advising its staff on the distinction between acceptable Americanisms ('teenage', 'babysitter', 'know-how', 'gimmick', 'stunt', 'commuter', 'blurb') and those which the Corporation advised against ('diaper', 'drug-store', 'sidewalk', 'transportation', 'hospitalize').

In some areas, the old British complaints about America have simply been deprived of all justification. On the question of service in shops and restaurants, nineteenth-century British visitors were continually irritated by the surliness and inattention of those paid to help them. Anyone visiting North America today would be unlikely to recognize this problem: unhelpful, grumpy service is now more often found at the check-out of a British supermarket than on the other side of the Atlantic. In Britain, servility has turned to apathy: the employee shrugs off the customer's concerns, and ignores the employer's interests. North American insolence, meanwhile, has been replaced by a pride in, and identification with, the job: there's an energy and a confidence about those who serve the public which is rarely matched in Britain.

Of the British habit of reporting home from America with casual, inaccurate observations, there seems, according to Americans, to be no end. The American journalist Cosmo Landesman (*Sunday Times*, 5 December 1993) complained about the 'growing taste for . . . books and television programmes portraying America as the land of the freak and the home of the bizarre'. Certainly the colourful 'only in America' story has long been a regular ingredient of British newspaper and broadcast journalism. A review by Laszlo Buhasz in the Canadian *Globe and Mail* (19 June 1993) even suggests there is still a tradition of itinerant Britons causing offence with their American memoirs. Buhasz found a new book by the British writer Pete Davies 'typical of the hit-and-run style of writing employed by many British writers when they do travel books about the United States'.

BIBLIOGRAPHY

Place of publication given only if outside London.

Arnold, Matthew, 'A Word about America' (essay), 1882, reprinted in *The Complete Prose Works of Matthew Arnold: Philistinism in England and America*, ed. R.H. Super, University of Michigan Press, 1974.
Barneby, W. Henry, *Life and Labour in the Far, Far West, being notes of a tour in the Western States, British Columbia, Manitoba, and the North-West Territory*, Cassell and Co., 1884.
Bird, Isabella, *The Englishwoman in America* (1856), *A Lady's Life in the Rocky Mountains*, John Murray, 1879.
Bodichon, Barbara, *An American Diary 1857–8*, Routledge & Kegan Paul, 1972.
Borrett, George Tuthill, *Out West, a series of Letters from Canada and the United States*, Groombridge and Sons, 1866.
Bromley, Clara Fitzroy, *A Woman's Wanderings in the Western World*, Saunders, Otley, and Co., 1861.
Burland, Rebecca, *A True Picture of Emigration*, 1848.
Burton, Sir Richard Francis, *The City of the Saints, and Across the Rocky Mountains to California*, Harper, New York; Longman, Green, Longman & Roberts, 1862.
Carbutt, Mrs E.H., *Five Months' Fine Weather in Canada, Western U.S., and Mexico*, Sampson, Low, Marston, Searle, & Rivington, 1889.
Cobbett, William, *Journal of a Year's Residence in the United States of America*, 1819.
Dickens, Charles, *American Notes for General Circulation*, Chapman and Hall, 1842.
Dixon, James, *Personal Narrative of a Tour Through a Part of the United States and Canada; with notices of the history and institutions of Methodism in America*, Lane and Scott, New York, 1849.
Fearon, Henry Bradshaw, *Sketches of America*, Longman, Hurst, Rees, Orme & Brown, 1818.
Fidler, Revd Isaac, *Observations on Professions, Literature, Manners and Emigration in the United States and Canada, made during a residence there in 1832*, 1833.
Guest, Lady Theodora, *A Round Trip in North America*, Edward Stanford, 1895.
Hall, Captain Basil, *Travels in North America*, Cadell, Edinburgh; Simpkin and Marshall, 1829.
Hamilton, Thomas, *Men and Manners in America*, Edinburgh, 1833.
Head, Sir Francis Bond, *The Emigrant*, John Murray, 1846.
Jameson, Anna Brownell, *Winter Studies and Summer Rambles*, Saunders and Ottley, 1838.
Johnson, R. Byron, *Very Far West Indeed*, Sampson, Low, Marston, Low & Searle, 1872.
Kemble, Fanny (Butler), *Journal of a Residence on a Georgian Plantation*, Harper and Brothers, New York; Longman and Company, 1863.
Kingsley, Charles, *His letters and memories of his life, Volume II*, Henry S. King & Co., 1877.
Kipling, Rudyard, *From Sea to Sea and other Sketches*, Macmillan, 1899. *Letters to the Family*, Macmillan, Toronto, 1908.
Langton, Anne, *A Gentlewoman in Upper Canada*, Irwin Publishing Inc, Toronto, 1950.
Langton, John, *Early Days in Upper Canada*, ed. W.A. Langton, The Macmillan Company of Canada, Toronto, 1926.
Mackay, Alexander, *The Western World; or Travels in the United States in 1846–7*, Bentley, 1850.
Mackay, Charles, *Life and Liberty in America: or Sketches of a tour in the United States and Canada in 1857–8*, Smith, Elder and Co., 1859.

Marryat, Captain Frederick, *A Diary in America, with Remarks on Its Institutions*, Longman, Orme, Green & Longmans, 1839.

Martineau, Harriet, *Society in America*, Saunders and Otley, 1837. *A Retrospect of Western Travel*, Saunders and Otley, 1838. *Autobiography*, Smith, Elder, & Co., 1877.

Maury, Sarah Mytton, *An Englishwoman in America*, Thomas Richardson and Son, 1848.

Moodie, Susanna, *Roughing it in the Bush*, Richard Bentley, 1852. *Life in the Clearings vs. the Bush*, Richard Bentley, 1853.

Murray, Hon Amelia M., *Letters from the United States, Cuba and Canada*, J.W.Parker & Son, G.P.Putnam & Co., New York, 1856.

Need, Thomas, *Six Years in the Bush, or Extracts from the Journal of a Settler in Upper Canada, 1832–1838*, Simpkin Marshall & Co., 1838.

Power, Tyrone Power, *Impressions of America during the Years 1833, 1834 and 1835*, 1836

Rae, William Fraser, *Westward by Rail, the New Route to the East*, Longmans, Green & Co., 1870.

Rhys, Captain Charles Horton, *A Theatrical Trip for a Wager*, 1861.

Ritchie, J. Ewing, *To Canada with Emigrants, A Record of Actual Experiences*, T. Fisher Unwin, 1885.

Roper, Edward, *By Track and Trail, a Journey through Canada*, W.H. Allen & Co. Ltd., 1891.

Russell, Bertrand, *Autobiography*, George Allen and Unwin Ltd., 1967.

Shaw, William, *Golden Dreams and Waking Realities; being the Adventures of a Gold-Seeker in California and the Pacific Islands*, Smith, Elder and Co., 1851.

Stevenson, Robert Louis, *The Silverado Squatters*, Chatto and Windus, 1883. *The Old Pacific Capital*, Charles Scribner's Sons, New York, 1892. *The Amateur Emigrant*, Chatto and Windus, 1895.

Sullivan, Edward, *Rambles and Scrambles in North and South America*, Richard Bentley, 1852.

Thackeray, William Makepeace, *The Letters and Private Papers of William Makepeace Thackeray, Vol 3: 1853–1856*, ed. Gordon N.Ray, Harvard University Press, Cambridge, Mass., 1946.

Thomson, William, *A Tradesman's Travels in the United States and Canada, in the Years 1840, 41 & 42*, Edinburgh, 1842.

Traill, Catherine Parr, *The Backwoods of Canada*, 1836. *The Canadian Settler's Guide*, Old Countryman, Toronto, 1855

Trollope, Anthony, *North America*, Chapman and Hall, 1862

Trollope, Fanny, *Domestic Manners of the Americans*, Whittaker and Treacher, 1832.

Trotter, Isabella (Strange), *First impressions of the new world on two travellers from the old in the autumn of 1858*, Longman, Brown, Green, Longmans & Roberts, 1859.

Weld, Charles, Richard, *A Vacation Tour in the United States and Canada*, Longman, Brown, Green and Longmans, 1855.

Wilde, Oscar, 'Impressions of America' (essay), 1883. 'The American Invasion' (essay), 1887. *Selected Letters of Oscar Wilde*, ed. Rupert Hart-Davis, Oxford University Press, Oxford, 1979.

Wright, Frances, *Views of Society and Manners in America*, Longman, Hurst, Rees, Orme, and Brown, 1821.

Picture and Copyright Credits

The author and publishers wish to thank the following for their kind permission to reproduce illustrations:

Bennett Studio Foundation, pp. 47, 50, 53, 131, 169; the Bettmann Archive, pp. 11, 83, 85, 87; Denver Public Library, pp. 45, 119; Historical Society of Washington, DC, p. 114; Hulton Deutsch Collection, pp. 21, 110, 116, 128, 139, 143, 145, 148, 150, 156, 162, 184; Huntingdon Library, pp. 65, 181; Mander and Mitchenson, p. 103; Mary Evans Picture Library, pp. 9, 56, 172; Museum of the City of New York, pp. 2, 4, 13, 17, 22, 28, 35, 38, 124, 125, 136; National Archives of Canada, pp. 77, 78; Nebraska State Historical Society, p. 74; New York Historical Society, pp. 31, 105, 111, 135; Peter Newark's Western Americana, pp. 24, 41, 63, 71, 101; Royal Geographical Society, p. 58; Smithsonian Institution, pp. 91, 93, 95, 98.

The following writers are quoted with the kind permission of their publishers:

Barbara Leigh Smith Bodichon from *An American Diary*, edited by Joseph W. Reed, Jr., published by Routledge and Kegan Paul in 1972.
Anne Langton, from *A Gentlewoman in Upper Canada*, published by General Publishing, Toronto, Ontario, Canada in 1964.
Bertrand Russell from his *Autobiography*, published by Unwin Hyman in 1967.
William Makepeace Thackeray from *The Letters of William Makepeace Thackeray*, edited by Gordon N. Ray, published by Harvard University Press in 1946.
Oscar Wilde from *Selected Letters of Oscar Wilde*, edited by Rupert Hart-Davies, published by Oxford University Press in 1979.

Index

accent, American, 38–9
Alaska, 89
appearance of Americans, 1–6
Arnold, Matthew, 40, 65, 112, 186

Baltimore, Maryland, 8, 100, 138
bar, 24
Barneby, W. Henry, 53, 160, 161, 165, 182, 186
Belleville, Ontario, 79, 187
Berkeley University, 189
Bird, Isabella, 49, 57, 58, 63, 64, 94, 97–8, 127, 132, 163, 164, 180
Bodichon, Barbara, 29, 55, 57, 66, 67, 108, 109, 111, 183, 186, 190
Borrett, George Tuthill, vi, 10, 43, 47, 146, 158, 186
Boston, Massachusetts, 9, 26, 39, 45, 137–8, 180
breakfast, 19
Britain, 12, 14–18, 112, 146, 175, 177–80, 183–5, 195–6
British Columbia, 160, 186, 188
Bromley, Clara Fitzroy, 10, 26, 51, 120, 139–40, 144, 150, 186
Buffalo, New York, 67–8, 157, 158, 159
Burland, Rebecca, 15, 60, 83, 186

Burton, Sir Richard Francis, 25, 96–7, 187

Calgary, Alberta, 53, 160
California, 25, 41, 153, 163–5, 174, 176
Canada, xi, 5, 8, 15, 21, 29, 30, 43, 44, 47, 66–8, 70–2, 120, 143–52, 159–61, 171, 176, 179–80, 182, 187
Carbutt, E.H., 120, 161, 165, 187
Chicago, Illinois, 154–7
children, 55–7
Cincinnati, Ohio, 8, 46, 114, 129, 153, 155, 157, 171, 176, 177
Cleveland, Ohio, 157, 158
Cobbett, William, xi, 187
Colorado Springs, Colorado, 57
Columbus, Ohio, 44
Congress, 112–14
conversation, 52, 129–30

Dana, Richard, 8, 176
death, 57, 58, 195
democracy, 112, 117, 175, 195
Democratic Party, 34
Denver, Colorado, 186
Detroit, Michigan, 157–8
Dickens, Charles, xi, 8, 9, 23, 38, 39, 45, 49, 50, 52, 70, 84, 88, 90, 99, 100–1, 104, 105, 109, 113, 115, 121, 134, 137–8, 140, 141–2, 144, 151, 154, 157, 180, 181–2, 184–5
Dixon, James, 66, 115, 150–1, 171, 182–3, 187
dinner, 20
drink, 23–6

emigrants, 69–70

Fearon, Henry Bradshaw, 1, 7, 16, 25, 33, 59, 69, 72, 98–9, 128, 137, 139, 187
Fidler, Revd Isaac, 71, 187
food, xi, 19–20, 22–3, 52, 55, 56, 115

Georgia, 102, 106, 175
Guest, Lady Theodora, xi, 29, 57, 94–5, 99, 138, 188

Hall, Captain Basil, 3, 12–14, 16, 23, 33, 34, 40, 83–4, 86, 88, 109, 113, 147, 151, 168, 169, 188
Head, Sir Francis Bond, 15, 188
Halifax, Nova Scotia, 144
Hamilton, Ontario, 146
Hamilton, Captain Thomas, 3, 4, 6, 10, 16, 19–20, 22, 34, 35, 39, 42, 45, 59, 61–2, 114–15, 123–6, 129, 137, 139, 147, 168, 170, 188

INDEX

Hartford, Connecticut, 170
hotels, 26–32

Illinois, 15, 61, 186–7
Indiana, 60, 61
Indians, American, 40, 72, 90–9
Irving, Washington, 9

Jackson, General Andrew, 34, 114–17
Jameson, Anna Brownell, 72, 92–3, 96, 148, 151–2, 153–4, 157, 180, 188
Johnson, R. Byron, 26, 31–2, 161–4, 182, 188

Kemble, Fanny, 30, 55, 101–3, 106, 107, 109–11, 147
Kentucky, 37, 61, 107
Kingsley, Charles, 4, 88, 164, 180, 189
Kipling, Rudyard, 1, 23, 27, 38, 68, 88–9, 123, 127, 145, 153, 159, 160, 163, 189

Lake Erie, 44, 48
Lake Huron, 92
Lake Tahoe, 49, 164
Langton, Anne, 70–1, 78, 121, 132, 189
Langton, John, 70, 74, 121, 189
language, 33–42, 195
Locke, John, 40
London, England, 14, 21, 146, 184
London, Ontario, 146
Longfellow, Henry Wadsworth, 8
Los Angeles, California, 165, 176, 186
Lowell, James Russell, 8, 112

Mackay, Alexander, 11, 12, 18, 65, 112, 121–2, 123–5, 130, 171, 174, 189
Mackay, Charles, 35, 39, 88, 100, 104, 134, 147, 153, 189
manners, 6–8, 10–12
Marryat, Captain Frederick, 3, 5, 7, 17, 23–4, 26, 29, 33, 36–8, 40, 44, 47, 48, 51, 57, 61, 66, 67, 69, 73–4, 84, 86, 87, 91, 97, 112, 115–18, 123, 125, 127, 130, 132, 137, 141, 142, 149, 157, 159, 167, 171, 176, 189–90
Martineau, Harriet, 12, 127, 181, 182, 190
Maryland, 125
Maury, Sarah Mytton, 26, 69, 106, 108, 126, 127, 190
Mexico, 164–5
Michigan, 61
Milwaukee, Wisconsin, 157, 158–9
Missouri, river, 64
Missouri, state of, 61
Mobile, Alabama, 55
Monroe, James, 115
Monterey, California, 164–5
Montreal, Quebec, 15, 29, 47, 145–6
Moodie, Susanna, 5, 30, 55, 76–7, 79–80, 82, 85, 94, 98, 121, 125, 130, 144, 148, 154, 171, 179–80
Murray, Hon. Amelia M., 7, 104, 108, 115, 147, 190

Nebraska, 87
Need, Thomas, 75, 79, 82–3, 90, 95, 120–1, 190

Nevada, 49
New England, 39, 45, 61–2, 125
New York, city of, xi, 1–7, 19, 29, 39, 133–7, 167, 173–4, 177
New York, state of, 59
New Orleans, 100, 176
Niagara Falls, xi, 7, 88, 147–52
North Carolina, 30

Ohio, 57, 61
Ontario, 93, 94, 121, 147, 190
Osbourne, Fanny, 6, 41

Pacific Railway, 44
Pennsylvania, 84, 125
Philadelphia, Pennsylvania, xi, 14, 59, 69, 102, 126, 139–41, 191
Pierce, General Franklin, 115
Pittsburgh, Pennsylvania, 57, 114, 187
place-names, 40, 42
Polk, James, 115
Portland, Maine, 142–3
Power, Tyrone, 61–2, 64, 129, 145, 171, 190
prairies, 86–8
Providence, Rhode Island, 45
public opinion, 44

Quakers, 59, 139–41, 191
Quebec City, Quebec, 47, 144–5

Rae, William Fraser, 16, 25, 29, 36, 39, 44, 45, 51, 155, 161–2, 164, 171, 174, 176, 191

religion, 59–61
Reno, Nevada, 51
Rhys, Captain Horton, 15, 26–7, 119–20, 126, 135, 146, 149, 180, 191
Ritchie, J. Ewing, 76, 191
Rochester, New York, 84
roads, 44–6
Roper, Edward, 159, 160, 161, 191
Rocky Mountains, 49, 58, 64
Russell, Bertrand, 118, 183, 191
Russell, William Howard, 5, 29, 31, 136

Sacramento, California, 25
Salt Lake City, Utah, 51, 94, 96, 187
San Diego, California, 165–6
San Francisco, California, 27, 41, 52, 68, 161–4, 176
servants, 118–22
Shaw, William, 165–6, 191
slavery, 66, 100–9, 190, 191
South, American, 39, 65–6, 104, 175
St Louis, Missouri, 39, 153, 186
St Paul, Minnesota, 157, 159
steamboats, 47–9
Stevenson, Robert Louis, 2, 6, 41, 42, 52, 54, 84–8, 95, 133, 154–5, 161, 165, 177

Sullivan, Edward, 13, 48–9, 117, 183, 191

Thackeray, William Makepeace, 101, 102, 104, 167, 191
Thomson, William, 76, 191
Thoreau, Henry, 15
Toronto, Ontario, 67–8, 72, 78, 92, 153–4, 187, 188
Traill, Catherine Parr, 8, 44–5, 72, 75, 77, 82, 93, 132, 146, 178–9
trains, xi, 8, 46, 49–54, 118, 127–8, 177–8
trees, 82–4
Trenton Falls, New York, 88
Trollope, Anthony, 2, 6, 14, 19, 20, 21, 27–8, 43, 56–7, 59, 62–4, 82, 102, 104, 114, 118, 122, 127–9, 134, 135–6, 138, 142, 146, 147, 149–50, 154, 157–60, 173, 174, 175, 180, 184
Trollope, Fanny, 4, 5, 8, 14, 22–3, 26, 28, 57, 60–1, 74, 81–2, 96, 100, 106, 108, 113–14, 116–17, 122, 126–7, 129, 133, 134, 138, 140, 142, 143, 149, 155, 171, 172, 173, 177, 184, 192
Trotter, Isabella Strange, 29, 34, 52, 107, 192

Truckee, California, 49
Tyler, John, 115

Utah, 49, 174

Van Buren, Martin, 115–16
Vancouver, British Columbia, 68, 160, 161
Vermont, 189
Victoria, British Columbia, 31, 160–1
Virginia, 34, 37, 104, 106, 125

Washington, DC, 114–16, 133, 141–2, 173–4
weather, 15–18
Weld, Charles Richard, 12, 15, 26, 46, 51, 59, 82, 107, 115, 155, 157, 176, 192
West, American, 39, 62–4, 164
White House, 116
Wilde, Oscar, 40, 56, 57, 64–5, 90, 124, 129, 148, 156, 164, 167, 177, 183, 192
Winnipeg, Manitoba, 159
women, 72, 78, 123–32
Wright, Frances, 40, 82, 118–19, 126, 127, 140, 145, 148–9, 168, 170, 192

Yellowstone National Park, Wyoming, 88–9